Chinese Food

MADE EASY

CHING-HE HUANG

Chinese Food
MADE EASY

📖 HarperCollins*Publishers*

HarperCollins*Publishers*
77–85 Fulham Palace Road
Hammersmith, London W6 8JB
www.harpercollins.co.uk

First published by HarperCollins in 2008

10 9 8 7 6 5 4 3 2 1

Text © Ching-He Huang 2008

Photographs © Kate Whitaker 2008
Styling: Wei Tang
Food styling: Annie Nichols

A catalogue record of this book is
available from the British Library

ISBN-13 978-0-00-726498-8
ISBN-10 0-00-726498-4

Printed and bound in China by
Leo Paper Products Ltd

This book includes references to nuts and recipes including nuts,
nut derivatives and nut oils. Avoid if you have a known allergic
reaction. Pregnant and nursing mothers, invalids, the elderly,
children and babies may be potentially vulnerable to nut allergies
and should therefore avoid nuts, nut derivatives and nut oils.

This book accompanies the BBC TWO series, *Chinese Food Made
Easy*, commissioned by Ben Gale and Lisa Edwards from Lion
Television Ltd and broadcast in 2008.
Executive Producers: Jeremy Mills and Richard Shaw
Director: David Robertson

BBC logo is copyright and trademark of the British Broadcasting
Corporation and is used under licence. BBC logo © BBC 1996.

Contents

Notes from a Chinese kitchen

FACT: TRADITIONAL CHINESE COOKING IS HEALTHY

When I first started to forge my TV career, it was difficult to break down the general perception that Chinese cuisine is unhealthy and bad for you. When most people in the UK think about Chinese food they almost always think of the local takeaways, some which are good but many of which are not. Monosodium glutamate (MSG), gloopy sugary sauces, deep-fried dishes laced with fat and salt – all dressed up as tasty, but in fact detrimental to one's health. There are over 15,000 Chinese restaurants and takeaways in the UK, and some unfortunately perpetuate this image, but my hope is to dispel this notion and set the record straight.

With their research into thousands of years of Chinese history, historians confirm that Chinese culture derived from its food culture. Chinese are obsessed with food. For centuries, peasants and farmers struggled against famine, poor harvests, and floods. Out of this struggle, cooking techniques such as wok frying were invented, and preserving techniques such as drying, pickling and curing followed. To the Chinese, the genius of all inventions is the wok; the shape of it allows the food to be cooked on a very high heat with very little oil, and with rapid stirring and tossing, the wok cooks the food to perfection. This way of cooking sears the food on the outside, not only helping to create a slight smoky flavour but also retaining the nutrients in the ingredients for optimum health. The wok is also used for steaming (with the help of the bamboo steamer) as well as for braising, smoking and making soups – all healthy cooking techniques.

In fact, traditionally, when Chinese families go out to eat at a Chinese restaurant, just one fried dish, or none at all, will accompany the series of dishes ordered to be shared at the table. This was very much the case in my family, when I first grew up with my grandmother. In her kitchen, she would only ever deep-fry food if it was on its last few days of freshness! This method is a safe way of cooking leftover ingredients by heating them in hot oil and therefore killing off any possible bacteria (although if you think of this fact every time you eat fried food, it may just put you off). My grandmother was seriously opposed to ordering fried fish in restaurants – it implied the fish was not fresh and she would always insist on having it steamed instead. If the fish was not fresh, it would be overly fishy once cooked, because fresh

fish when steamed should be odourless. However, I am not as strict as my grandmother when it comes to cooking or consuming fried foods. Of course, I would hope that all restaurants and takeaways use the freshest ingredients. To ensure that you are eating healthily, my advice is to cook the food yourself; and if you are dining out, then remember that keeping the balance right is key to good health and enjoying any cuisine – never too much of one thing is best for you.

In terms of balance, another important aspect of Chinese food is the philosophy of 'yin' and 'yang' – this is one of the foundations and principles of Chinese cooking. The belief is that all food has a 'yin' and a 'yang' element attached to it – 'yin' foods are cooling and 'yang' foods are heat giving. Traditionally, Chinese cooks would try to balance these foods in any one dish. 'Yin' foods include cucumber, fruits and most vegetables, while 'yang' foods are most meats, ginger, garlic and chillies. So a perfectly balanced dish might have a balance of meat and vegetables. Cooking techniques also impart a 'yin' or 'yang' element to a dish. Stir-frying and steaming are 'yin', whereas deep-frying is 'yang' – so if you deep-fry some vegetables, the dish is balanced overall because the vegetables are 'yin' and deep-frying is 'yang'.

This philosophy not only applies to food in Chinese culture, but also in Feng shui (the practice of creating harmony in the home) and in Traditional Chinese Medicine, with which practitioners, by using certain foods, help heal the body of illnesses caused by imbalances in one's lifestyle. Chinese believe that food is medicine for the body, mind and soul.

MY KIND OF FOOD

With this in mind, I have created dishes in this book that may sound familiar but that have a modern twist in cooking techniques or ingredients. Some of the dishes are new versions of old favourites, and some are traditional recipes I have collected from my travels in China, simplified to demonstrate how healthy, light and simple Chinese cooking can be. Some of these dishes were the result of working with farmers, producers and the British public from all walks of life, who inspired me to re-create recipes that suited their working and home lifestyles – Richard, for example, who needed my help to convince the town of Chorley to buy his local, home-grown chillies, and Robbie, who wanted some new healthy recipes to cook for his watch at the Blackburn fire brigade. The recipes are wide ranging, varied and versatile.

From Takeaway Favourites, I love my healthier version of Sweet and sour pork and also my Sweet and tangy chilli beef (which may come as a surprise to many Chinese as it involves eating raw pak choy leaves – traditionally, Chinese don't like eating cold raw vegetable dishes. But for health, I think we can take the best of both cultures and create the ideal balance of East and West).

My Spicy Sichuan dishes may surprise but, I hope, also inspire you; these dishes are for chilli lovers – try the Spicy hotpot! You can go to town with them and vary the degree of heat to your liking. Many dishes are my simpler takes on the traditional, such as Dan Dan noodles, Sichuan orange beef, Bang-Bang chicken and Spicy warm bacon or lardon and cucumber salad. For vegetarians who love dofu, try my Spicy dofu and edamame beans.

For those who love getting their hands dirty, the Dumplings, Dim Sum and Noodles chapter is for you – lots of rolling, folding and stuffing. Try my Wonton noodle soup, Roast pork pastry puffs, Pork and prawn dumplings, or my favourite noodle recipe of all time, 'Dragon Prawn' noodles. These types of dishes are great for a dim sum or cocktail party.

For seafood lovers, check out the Cleansing clam and daikon soup in Fish and Seafood – light and delicious, this was one of my grandmother's recipes. Another Huang family favourite is my Mum's lobster and mayo brioche, which is not Chinese but so good that I wanted to share it with you! My recipe for Black bean steamed scallops with noodles was inspired by the best seafood in Hong Kong and it won't disappoint. For a great comforting dish, it has to be my Seafood congee – if you like seafood risotto then do give this recipe a whirl! To impress, try the Coriander prawns and Longjing tea – it is finger-licking good, even if I do say so myself!

For a quick snack explore the Street Food chapter and try my Spiced beef stir-fry topped with spring onion, stuffed in wheat flour tortillas or steamed pancakes, and served with a dollop of wasabi mayo – this is a real fusion snack and delicious. Or try the healthy version of my Chicken and vegetable spring rolls.

The Celebration Food chapter has all the dishes I love serving to family and friends. These dishes are more traditional in terms of flavour, such as my Lionhead meatballs, Drunken chicken, Steamed egg, shiitake mushrooms and seaweed, Buddha's stir-fried vegetables and Northern-style bean curd. There are some twists, too – try the Steamed sea bass in hot beer and ginger lime sauce and the Lamb chops in dofu ru with adzuki and butter bean mash.

In my family, we usually have fresh citrus fruits after a meal to help cleanse the palate, but I just adore desserts. So I couldn't help but create some light refreshing ones to share with you. Perhaps Durian honey puffs with vanilla ice cream and maple syrup will appeal, or Fruity sticky rice with toffee sauce, Mango madness, Red bean paste and banana spring rolls, Lychee lime and mixed fruit jelly or Empress Dowager Cixi's longevity peach pudding might tempt you to get cooking in the kitchen?

CHINA AND CHINESE CULTURE: MY ENDLESS SOURCES OF INSPIRATION

So far in my food career I have been fortunate to meet and swap tips with cooks, chefs, foodies and people from all walks of life who have a tremendous appetite for good food, and I hope long may these experiences and exchanges continue because I am enriched by them. I feel very lucky to have travelled in China recently and to have seen it go through a very exciting transformation. With China hosting the forthcoming Beijing Olympics, the world's attention will be focused on all things Chinese for those few weeks, and for this I am grateful. I am pleased that it will allow China to show off its rich and beautiful culture, open its doors and share it with the world. There's never been a better time to get excited about China, so whether it's food, culture or language that you are interested in – go for it!

Food, to Chinese people, means many different things and it is the cultural heart and soul of China. Food is of such social and economic importance that the Chinese language and common phrases are founded almost solely to express this importance. When I studied Chinese at Sunday school (forced by my parents but now I am so glad I did), I learnt phrases that express how important food is. During the Chinese New Year, we would have a meal called 'Tuan yuan fan' (Togetherness rice/meal), which is used to express the idea of families getting together to eat on this special occasion. In Beijing, when you lose your job, they have a saying, 'Da puo le fan guo' (You've broken the rice bowl, or in other words, you've lost your wages in terms of food).

Whenever I eat with friends or family in China, the hospitality never ceases to amaze me. It is the 'E-e' (meaning) behind the gestures and the character and symbolism of the food that is significant. I really believe that to understand Chinese culture you must start by learning Chinese food culture. For example, when holding a banquet, the number of dishes ordered and the quality and cost of the ingredients should be taken into consideration – be sure not to under-order or you will seem money-pinching, and be sure not to over-order or you may be considered a show-off. The Chinese communicate through eating. A well ordered banquet meal can be considered real 'kung fu' – the skill in achieving the right balance and yet appearing humble and modest to your guests. (Never fear, if you ever find yourself in a banquet situation just remember to be yourself and that all acts of love are universally appreciated.)

As I was growing up, my mother, when preparing a meal, would always make reference to the fact that she had spent hours making a certain dish or how she had had to go to a special outlet to get an ingredient, and so on. I used to think we were such a burden to her. But now I understand she wasn't trying to make us feel bad, rather that it was her way of communicating and expressing how much she loved us; she showed it through the time and difficulty it took to prepare the dishes – the labour of love!

This 'love' can be found throughout Chinese history in the kitchens of the imperial courts of the dynasties that ruled China over the centuries. The love for the emperor was shown by the number of dishes prepared for a meal – I was told that the late Empress Dowager Cixi (of the last Qing dynasty) would have on a daily basis over 108 dishes cooked for her in a one-meal sitting. And that in the emperor's court there were more food and wine staff than any other staff (apart from the Emperor's armies, of course). A lot of the inspiration behind imperial cuisine related to the preparation, time and skill required to cook a dish – fish eyes are a delicacy not because of their flavour but because of the amount of fish that has to be caught to make a dish full of them! When your Chinese friends take you out and lavish you with their hospitality, it's their way of saying they love you!

I continue to learn about my heritage every day. My culinary passions are kept alive by the wealth of truths and traditions in my culture, which I am pleased to be able to share and introduce a little to you through my recipes.

COOK FROM THE HEART

Cooking and eating wonderful food every day to me is pure joy and a sign of our wealth. This does not mean that every dish need be extravagant or expensive – a well-cooked stir-fry or fried rice can give great satisfaction. In my opinion, often the best-tasting dishes are those simple classics cooked from the heart and given plenty of love and attention.

Happy reading, cooking, eating and sharing. I hope this book will inspire you to travel to China and sample some of the wonderful delights as I have. But moreover, I hope it will get you cooking delicious Chinese food in the comfort of your home. The most important tips I can offer in cooking are to relax, enjoy the experience, make the dish yours, and practice makes perfect.

'Kumpei' (bottoms up) to 'Sheng ti jian kung' (good health), 'Kwai le' (happiness) and cooking from the heart with 'Ai' (love).

With love and happy wokking,

Takeaway favourites

This is a variation on sweet and sour soy sticky ribs, which are traditionally braised in stock and then the sauce is added and thickened. However, I marinate pork fillet slices in homemade sweet and sour sauce, wok-fry them until sticky and stuff them in griddled seeded buns with caramelised red onions and salad leaves. In my opinion, this is the ultimate party food.

Sweet and sour soy pork buns

SERVES 4

600g/1lb 5oz piece of pork fillet
1 garlic clove, finely chopped
2 tablespoons yellow bean sauce
1 tablespoon Shaohsing rice wine or dry
   sherry
3 tablespoons groundnut oil

FOR THE SWEET AND SOUR SAUCE

2 tablespoons light soy sauce
2 tablespoons Chinkiang black rice
   vinegar or balsamic vinegar
1 tablespoon soft light brown sugar
2 tablespoons runny honey

1 pinch each of sea salt and ground white
   pepper

FOR THE CARAMELISED RED ONIONS

1 tablespoon groundnut oil
3 red onions, sliced
1 tablespoon Chinkiang black rice vinegar
   or balsamic vinegar
1 tablespoon soft light brown sugar

TO SERVE

8 large sesame-seeded buns
green and red lollo salad leaves, washed
   and shredded
some beef tomato slices (optional)

1 Put the pork, garlic, yellow bean sauce and rice wine or sherry into a large bowl, add all the ingredients for the sweet and sour sauce and stir to combine. Cover and place in the fridge to marinate for as long as possible – overnight is ideal. When ready to cook, drain the pork, retaining the marinade, and cut into thin slices. Heat a wok over a high heat and add 2 tablespoons groundnut oil. Stir-fry the pork for 3–4 minutes until browned. Add the marinade, reduce the heat and cook for 2–3 minutes until the sauce has a sticky consistency.

2 To make the caramelised onions, heat a small pan, add the groundnut oil and stir-fry the onions for 4–5 minutes until softened. Add the vinegar and sugar and cook for 1 minute to caramelise.

3 Heat a griddle pan and add 1 tablespoon groundnut oil. Cut each bun in half, place in the pan, cut side down, and cook until slightly browned.

4 To serve, stuff each bun with salad leaves, some sticky pork slices, caramelised onions and tomato slices, if you like, and serve immediately.

The secret to making the chicken extra tasty is to coat it in egg white and cornflour and then shallow-fry it to give it a crispy coating. However, if you are pushed for time, just add the raw chicken after the onion in the stir-fry and fry until it turns opaque, and then add the rest of the ingredients.

Chicken and cashew nut stir-fry

SERVES 4 TO SHARE

1 egg white
1 tablespoon cornflour
1 pinch of sea salt
500g/1lb 2oz skinless chicken breast fillets, sliced
300ml/10fl oz groundnut oil

FOR THE STIR-FRY

1 onion, sliced
1 yellow pepper, deseeded and sliced into strips
1 red pepper, deseeded and sliced into strips
3 tablespoons chicken stock
2–3 tablespoons light soy sauce
2 large spring onions, sliced
4 tablespoons roasted cashew nuts (or toast in a pan)
sea salt and ground white pepper
steamed jasmine rice (see page 156) to serve

1 Place the egg white in a bowl, add the cornflour and a pinch of salt and stir to combine. Add the chicken to the mixture and coat the chicken well.

2 Heat a wok over a high heat and add the groundnut oil. Fry the chicken until golden brown and crispy, then remove with a slotted spoon and drain on absorbent kitchen paper.

3 Pour off all but 1 tablespoon of oil from the wok. Reheat the oil over a high heat, add the onion and stir-fry for a few seconds. Add the yellow and red pepper slices and stir-fry for 1 minute until they have softened a little. Add the chicken pieces and stir-fry for 1 minute, then add the stock, soy sauce, salt and pepper.

4 Finally, add the spring onions and cashew nuts and stir well. Transfer to a serving dish and serve immediately with steamed rice.

Ching's tip

For an alternative, add some cooked egg noodles with the cashew nuts in step 4 and mix through for a chicken and cashew nut chow mein.

This is a recipe my grandmother and my mother would make using sticky glutinous rice. I use jasmine rice and it is equally delicious.

When cooked using glutinous rice (see Ching's tip), this chicken fried rice dish can be quite like 'You fan' (oiled rice). This may also remind you of the rice wrapped in lotus leaf or bamboo leaf you get as a dim sum. Now you can recreate it at home.

Grandmother's chicken fried rice

SERVES 4

2 tablespoons groundnut oil

1 tablespoon freshly grated root ginger

3 shallots, finely chopped

3 dried Chinese mushrooms, pre-soaked in hot water for 20 minutes, drained and finely chopped

225g/8oz skinless chicken breast fillets, finely diced

1 tablespoon Shaohsing rice wine or dry sherry

1 teaspoon five-spice powder

1 tablespoon dark soy sauce

50g/2oz dry-roasted peanuts

300g/11oz cooked jasmine rice (see page 156) or glutinous rice (see page 156)

3–4 tablespoons light soy sauce

1–2 tablespoons toasted sesame oil

ground white pepper

1 spring onion, finely chopped

1 Heat a wok or pan over a high heat and add the groundnut oil. Add the ginger, shallots and Chinese mushrooms and cook for a few seconds.

2 Add the chicken and cook for a minute or two, then add the rice wine or sherry followed by the five-spice powder. As the chicken starts to turn white, add the dark soy sauce.

3 Add the peanuts and then the rice, mix well and stir-fry for 1 minute.

4 Season with the light soy sauce, sesame oil and pepper to taste and stir to mix. Finally, stir in the spring onion, transfer to a serving dish and serve immediately.

Ching's tip
The authentic version of this recipe with glutinous rice gives a wonderful sticky texture, but the rice is not readily available in supermarkets, which is a shame. If you visit a Chinese supermarket, do look out for it.

I love my fried rice – this is the perfect dish to accompany stir-fried meat or vegetarian dishes. The earthy mushrooms are full of flavour and the tabasco gives this dish a delicious lift. If you don't like tabasco you can leave it out or add a few finely diced spicy-sweet pickled peppers.

Egg and shiitake mushroom fried rice with tabasco

SERVES 2

2 tablespoons groundnut oil
2 eggs, lightly beaten
100g/3½oz chestnut mushrooms and shiitake mushrooms, sliced
75g/3oz frozen green peas
200g/7oz steamed jasmine rice (see page 156) or cooked basmati rice
2 tablespoons light soy sauce
1 tablespoon toasted sesame oil
1 pinch of ground white pepper
a few splashes of tabasco sauce

1 Heat a wok over a high heat and add 1 tablespoon groundnut oil. Add the beaten eggs to the wok, stir to scramble, then remove and set aside.

2 Heat the remaining groundnut oil in the wok and add the mushrooms. Stir-fry for 1 minute, then add the frozen peas and stir-fry for less than 1 minute. Add the rice and mix well until the rice has broken down.

3 Return the egg to the wok and stir through, then season with soy sauce, sesame oil and a pinch of white pepper. Just before serving, season with tabasco sauce to taste.

Chilli chicken stir-fry with plenty of sauce is an easy, delicious recipe you can make at home without the use of bought-in sauces. It is chilli, tangy and sweet with plenty of heat from the ginger. Add some cooked noodles and the results are fabulous.

Chilli chicken with noodles

SERVES 2

150g/5oz dried yellow shi wheat flour noodles
groundnut oil
250g/9oz skinless chicken breast fillets, sliced
1 courgette, sliced into strips
½ red pepper, deseeded and sliced into strips
2 tablespoons light soy sauce
2 large spring onions, sliced lengthways

FOR THE SAUCE

4 garlic cloves, crushed and finely chopped
2.5cm/1 inch piece of fresh root ginger, peeled, sliced and finely chopped
1 medium red chilli, deseeded and finely chopped
½ red pepper, deseeded and sliced into strips
2 tomatoes, sliced
5 tablespoons water
2 tablespoons tomato ketchup
1 teaspoon soft light brown sugar

1 Place all the ingredients for the sauce into a blender and blitz.

2 Cook the noodles according to the packet instructions. Drain, then run them under cold running water and drain again. Drizzle with a little groundnut oil and put to one side.

3 Heat a wok over a high heat and add 1 tablespoon groundnut oil. Add the chicken and stir-fry for 2–3 minutes until it starts to turn brown. Add the courgette and red pepper and stir-fry together for 1 minute. Add the sauce and bring to the boil.

4 Add the cooked noodles and stir well to combine. Season with the soy sauce, garnish with the spring onions and serve immediately.

Ching's tip
This sauce is equally delicious served with steamed jasmine rice (see page 156).

I usually like to kick off 'takeaway'-themed dinners at home with a nourishing bowl of 'egg flower' drop soup. This was one of the very first dishes my mother taught me – it's a great way to pack all the nutrients you need into a one-pot, easy-to-make dish. I like it with plenty of spinach, too, for an extra health boost. This soup is not only good if you're watching the waistline, but it also tastes delicious. Omit the dofu and seaweed if you are not a fan. In Taiwan, takeaway restaurants offer steaming bowls of soup like this one to accompany your meal.

'Egg flower' drop soup

SERVES 2

**3 ripe tomatoes, sliced
(see step 1)**
**500ml/18fl oz hot vegetable
stock**
2 eggs, lightly beaten
1 tablespoon light soy sauce
a dash of sesame oil
**1 pinch of ground white
pepper**
**1 tablespoon cornflour
blended with 2 tablespoons
cold water**
**1–2 sheets nori (dried
seaweed), shredded**
**200g/7oz fresh silken dofu,
diced into 1.5 x 1.5cm/
½ x ½ inch chunks**
1 large handful of spinach
2 spring onions, finely sliced

1 If you want to skin the tomatoes before slicing, cut a cross at the base of each one. Plunge them into a pan of boiling water for less than 1 minute, then drain – the skin will peel off easily. Finely chop the flesh, discarding the hard centre. However, most of the nutrients are underneath the skin so I don't bother – also the dish is even quicker to prepare.

2 Add the tomatoes to the hot stock in the pan. Pour the whisked eggs into the broth, stirring gently. Add the soy sauce, sesame oil, pepper and blended cornflour and mix well.

3 Add the nori to the broth, followed by the dofu and heat for less than 1 minute.

4 Add the spinach and let it wilt slightly, then add the spring onions. Serve immediately.

This is my simple and healthy version of sweet and sour pork and will be unlike anything you have tasted in a Chinese restaurant. I hope it's one you will love to cook time and time again. Instead of the crunchy batter, the crunchy roasted soya beans give texture and flavour.

Sweet and sour pork

SERVES 2

2 pork loin chops or steaks
2 tablespoons groundnut oil
light soy sauce
a dash of Shaohsing rice wine
or dry sherry
ground white pepper
salad leaves or steamed
jasmine rice or Beijing rice
(see page 156) to serve

FOR THE PORK COATING

3 tablespoons roasted whole
soya beans or dry-roasted
peanuts
a pinch of sea salt (optional)
a few pinches of ground
white pepper
1 teaspoon crushed dried
chillies

FOR THE SWEET AND SOUR
SAUCE

125g/4oz tinned pineapple in
natural juice
125ml/4fl oz pineapple
juice
3 tablespoons freshly
squeezed lime juice

1 Put all the ingredients for the pork coating into a grinder and whiz until coarsely ground, or grind in a pestle and mortar. Transfer to a bowl. Put all the ingredients for the sweet and sour sauce into a blender and whiz to a paste.

2 Sprinkle the pork coating onto a board and press the pork into the spice mix, pressing down so that the mix sticks to the meat, and coating well on both sides.

3 Heat a wok or pan over a high heat and add the groundnut oil. Add the pork and cook for 2 minutes until browned, then turn over and cook the other side for 2 minutes, or until fully cooked. Remove the pork from the wok and put to one side in a warm place.

4 Pour the sweet and sour sauce into the wok and cook for 1–2 minutes until the sauce has reduced and thickened naturally. Season further if required with light soy sauce, rice wine or sherry, salt and pepper.

5 Serve the sauce poured over the pork, with salad leaves or rice.

Ching's tip
The Choi sum and mixed vegetable salad with pineapple dressing on page 162 would also go well with this dish.

This is a classic takeaway dish and a classic Chinese snack – Chow mein in Mandarin Chinese is pronounced 'chao meean' and it means 'stir-noodle', or stir-fried noodle.

I like this simple dish with plenty of fresh crunchy vegetables and light soy sauce and toasted sesame oil – but the key to a good chow mein is in the quality of the noodles. I use shi wheat flour noodles – 'shi' means 'thin' – and whether yellow shi or white, they are easy to cook, just 3 minutes in boiling water. Then all the ingredients go into a wok – couldn't be easier or healthier!

Chicken chow mein

SERVES 2

150g/5oz dried yellow shi wheat flour noodles
toasted sesame oil
300g/11oz skinless chicken breast fillets, sliced into strips
a dash of dark soy sauce
1 teaspoon five-spice powder
1 tablespoon cornflour
2 tablespoons groundnut oil
1 red pepper, deseeded and finely sliced
150g/5oz bean sprouts
1 large spring onion, sliced lengthways
2 tablespoons light soy sauce
1 teaspoon chilli sauce (optional)
finely ground black pepper (optional)

1 Cook the noodles for 3 minutes in a pan of boiling water until al dente. Drain, then run them under cold running water and drain again. Drizzle with a few splashes of sesame oil and toss through to prevent them from sticking.

2 Season the chicken with a splash of dark soy sauce and coat with the five-spice powder. Coat lightly with the cornflour.

3 Heat a wok over a high heat, add the groundnut oil and heat until smoking, then add the chicken and stir-fry for 2–3 minutes until cooked.

4 Add the red pepper and stir-fry for 1 minute, then add the bean sprouts and spring onion and stir-fry for less than 1 minute. Add the cooked noodles and season with the light soy sauce and 1 teaspoon sesame oil. If you like, stir in the chilli sauce and some black pepper. Stir well and serve immediately.

This dish is so simple to cook and eat. There's no need for the gloopy bought sauce laden with MSG – this home-made version is full of flavour and takes minutes to cook.

This is definitely one of my favourite suppers. A great accompaniment is cooked jasmine rice, but if I'm not in the mood for a large meal, I eat the dish with plenty of greens – wok-fried chilli pak choy. Or try my tangy Black vinegar oyster mushrooms (see page 166), which when topped on the beef give it an earthy, tangy edge.

Beef in oyster sauce

SERVES 2

350g/12oz fillet of beef
1 teaspoon light soy sauce
1 tablespoon oyster sauce
plus 1 teaspoon
1 pinch of sugar
2 tablespoons groundnut oil
3 garlic cloves, crushed and
finely chopped
1 medium chilli, deseeded
and finely chopped
200g/7oz baby white-
stemmed pak choy, sliced
in half
salt and ground black pepper

1 Prepare the fillet of beef by hammering it with a meat cleaver, the side of a Chinese cleaver or a rolling pin. Slice it thinly and place the pieces in a bowl. Season the beef with the soy sauce, 1 tablespoon oyster sauce, the sugar, salt and pepper. Set aside.

2 Heat a wok over a high heat and add 1 tablespoon groundnut oil. Add the garlic and chilli and toss quickly, then add the pak choy and stir-fry for 1 minute. Season with a pinch of salt and 1 teaspoon oyster sauce. Transfer the pak choy to a serving plate.

3 Heat the wok over a high heat and add the remaining groundnut oil. Add the beef slices and stir-fry for 1–2 minutes. To serve, either place the beef slices on the pak choy or toss the beef with the pak choy, then serve immediately.

I love deep-fried crispy chilli beef, but deep-frying is not always healthy. So I have come up with a light but tasty alternative that cooks the beef in a fast and furious way – in the wok!

This is another of my favourite fast, delicious, healthy suppers and I hope it gets your thumbs up. You can reduce the amount of sugar if you like.

Sweet and tangy chilli beef

SERVES 4

1 tablespoon groundnut oil
250g/9oz fillet of beef, cut into
  5mm/¼ inch strips
1 teaspoon Shaohsing rice wine
  or dry sherry
1 pinch of crushed dried chilli
  flakes
1 teaspoon light soy sauce
1 pinch of ground white pepper
1 large handful of baby spinach
  leaves, washed
2 heads of green-stemmed pak
  choy, washed and sliced
1 small mango, peeled, stoned
  and finely diced

FOR THE SWEET AND TANGY
DRESSING

1 tablespoon light soy sauce
4 tablespoons lemon juice
2 tablespoons orange juice
1 teaspoon groundnut oil
2 teaspoons caster sugar
1 tablespoon runny honey
⅓ cucumber, halved
  lengthways, deseeded and
  very finely chopped
1 medium green chilli, deseeded
  and very finely chopped

1 To make the sweet and tangy dressing, combine the soy sauce, lemon juice, orange juice, groundnut oil, caster sugar and honey in a bowl. Whisk to make the dressing and then add the cucumber and chilli. Stir and set aside.

2 Heat a wok over a high heat and add the groundnut oil. Add the beef to the wok and stir-fry quickly. Add the rice wine or sherry and cook for a few seconds. Add the chilli flakes, soy sauce and white pepper. Cook to your preference – less than a minute for medium, or a minute longer for well done.

3 Dress the serving plates with the spinach leaves and pak choy. Spoon some of the chilli beef in the middle, spoon generous amounts of the dressing over the top and sprinkle over some finely diced mango. Serve immediately.

'Mee-fun', or 'rice noodles', made their way to Singapore via travelling Fujianese Chinese traders – rice is predominantly grown in this sub-tropical Chinese province. On Singaporean soil, rice noodles were fused with ingredients like turmeric and curry powder used by other trading Indians and local Malays, and thus this delicious stir-fried rice noodle dish was born. It is a takeaway favourite all over the world and one of my favourite brunch dishes. The bacon is not traditional but is a good substitute for Chinese Char-siu roast pork. Don't let the long list of ingredients faze you, it's worth it to create the layers of flavours!

Singapore-style noodles

SERVES 2

2 tablespoons groundnut oil

1 tablespoon freshly grated root ginger

1 red chilli, deseeded and finely chopped

5 fresh shiitake mushrooms, sliced

1–2 tablespoons turmeric

175g/6oz raw tiger prawns, shelled and deveined

100g/3½oz diced smoked bacon

1 red pepper, deseeded and sliced

1 handful of julienne carrot strips

1 handful of bean sprouts

100g/3½oz cooked chicken breast, shredded

250g/9oz dried vermicelli rice noodles, pre-soaked in hot water for 10 minutes and drained

1 teaspoon crushed dried chillies

2 tablespoons light soy sauce

2 tablespoons oyster sauce

1 tablespoon clear rice vinegar or cider vinegar

1 egg, beaten

a dash of toasted sesame oil

2 spring onions, sliced lengthways

1 Heat the groundnut oil in a wok and stir-fry the ginger, chilli, mushrooms and turmeric for a few seconds.

2 Add the prawns and stir-fry for 1 minute until they start to turn pink, then add the bacon and cook for less than 1 minute. Add the rest of the vegetables and cook for 1 minute, then add the cooked chicken and stir well to combine.

3 Add the noodles and stir-fry for 2 minutes, then season with the chillies, soy sauce, oyster sauce and vinegar and stir to combine.

4 Add the beaten egg, stir gently until the egg is cooked through (less than 1 minute) and then season with sesame oil. Sprinkle with the spring onions and serve immediately.

Spicy Sichuan
dishes

This is a naughty starter – I like to marinate very fine shreds of pork in rice wine and then I dip them in cornflour and shallow-fry them until crispy. Once they are cooked, I sprinkle on a seasoning of spice mix and serve them on a salad. If you are not a fan of pork, you could use chicken, turkey or duck. If you are vegetarian, cut long thin strips of fresh bean curd, dust in some cornflour and shallow-fry until crisp, season with light soy sauce and then follow the rest of the recipe.

Sichuan crispy chilli pork on lettuce

SERVES 2

350g/12oz finely shredded pork fillet
1 teaspoon Shaohsing rice wine or dry sherry
4 tablespoons cornflour
200ml/7fl oz groundnut oil
1 small handful of dried vermicelli mung bean noodles
2–3 pinches of sea salt
2–3 pinches of ground black pepper
1–2 pinches of crushed dried chillies

TO SERVE

2 Little Gem lettuces, washed and leaves separated
1 small carrot, grated
½ cucumber, grated
1 small handful of bean sprouts, roughly chopped in half
1 small handful of fresh coriander, leaves and stalks, finely chopped
1 lime, cut into wedges

1 Put the pork fillet into a bowl, add the rice wine or sherry and marinate for 10 minutes. Just before cooking, add the cornflour and coat the pork shreds well.

2 Heat a shallow pan or small wok over a high heat and add the groundnut oil. Add the pork and stir-fry for 2 minutes until crispy, then drain on absorbent kitchen paper.

3 Add the mung bean noodles to the pan or wok and fry until doubled in size and opaque. Drain on absorbent kitchen paper.

4 Put the salt, pepper and crushed chillies into a bowl. Add the pork to the spice mix and turn to lightly coat.

5 Divide the lettuce leaves between two plates. Fill each with grated carrot, cucumber and bean sprouts, top with the crispy chilli pork and then some crispy mung bean noodles. Sprinkle with finely chopped coriander. To eat, drizzle each little parcel with lime juice and enjoy!

In Sichuan cooking, over twenty three different flavours can be created. 'Yu-shiang', or 'fish fragrant', is just one of these, but this dish does not actually taste 'fishy'. It is a way of describing the almost bouillon-like taste that is derived from using a good stock. Here, the flavour is created using a good chicken stock, chilli bean sauce and rice vinegar. I love cooking this dish time and time again. If you like your vegetables, slice some baby green-stemmed pak choy in half lengthways from leaf to stem, and add before the chicken stock.

Fish fragrant aubergine pork

SERVES 4 TO SHARE

3 tablespoons groundnut oil

1 aubergine, halved lengthways and then cut into 1cm/½ inch slices, top to bottom

2 garlic cloves, crushed and finely chopped

1 medium red chilli, deseeded and finely chopped

1 tablespoon freshly grated root ginger

200g/7oz minced pork

1 tablespoon Shaohsing rice wine or dry sherry

2 tablespoons chilli bean sauce

200ml/7fl oz hot chicken stock

1 tablespoon clear rice vinegar or cider vinegar

1 teaspoon toasted sesame oil

2 large spring onions, chopped

1 tablespoon cornflour blended with 2 tablespoons cold water

1 Heat a wok over a high heat and add 2 tablespoons groundnut oil. Add the aubergine slices and a few splashes of water to create some steam and fry until the aubergine is softened and golden on the outside. Transfer to a plate and put to one side.

2 Wipe out the wok, reheat and add 1 tablespoon groundnut oil. Stir-fry the garlic, chilli and ginger for a few seconds, then add the minced pork. Stir-fry for 1 minute, then add the rice wine or sherry. Cook until the meat is browned, then add the chilli bean sauce and stock. Return the aubergines to the wok.

3 Season with the vinegar and sesame oil and bring to the boil. Stir in the spring onions. Add the blended cornflour and stir to thicken. Serve immediately.

This famed Sichuan dish originated in Chengdu; the name comes from the bamboo shoulder poles (dan) from which the noodle sellers suspended their stoves, noodles and sauces. This is served as a quick solution to those in need of a snack — mah-jong players and gamblers wandering around the city at night — but I love to serve small bowls of it as a starter to get the tastebuds going. There are several versions, some spicier and some drier than others, but I like more sauce and have added chicken stock. Traditionally, this dish also uses preserved mustard greens or Tianjin preserved vegetables, but one day I didn't have any and used pickled cornichons instead.

Dan Dan noodles

SERVES 4

FOR THE MEAT TOPPING

2 tablespoons groundnut oil

2 garlic cloves, crushed and finely chopped

1 tablespoon freshly grated root ginger

1 medium red chilli, deseeded and finely chopped

250g/9oz minced beef

1 tablespoon Shaohsing rice wine or dry sherry

100g/3½oz cornichons or cocktail gherkins in vinegar, drained and finely diced

1 tablespoon light soy sauce

FOR THE NOODLE BASE AND SAUCE

500g/1lb 2oz any wheat flour noodles

toasted sesame oil

1 tablespoon sesame paste, or tahini blended with 1 teaspoon toasted sesame oil

1 tablespoon chilli oil

1 tablespoon Chinkiang black rice vinegar or balsamic vinegar

750ml/1¼ pints chicken stock

FOR THE GARNISH

1 teaspoon whole Sichuan peppercorns

1 large spring onion, finely chopped

1 small handful of fresh coriander, leaves and stalks, finely chopped

1 teaspoon chilli oil

1 teaspoon toasted sesame oil

For the method, please see overleaf.

1 Cook the noodles according to the packet instructions, drain and toss them through with some sesame oil. Put to one side.

2 To make the meat topping, heat a wok over a high heat and add the groundnut oil. Add the garlic, ginger and chilli and stir-fry for a few seconds, then add the minced beef. As the beef starts to turn brown, add the rice wine or sherry and cook for a few seconds. Stir in the cornichons or gherkins and cook until fragrant, then season with the soy sauce and keep on a very low heat.

3 Next, make the noodle sauce. Put the sesame paste or blended tahini, the chilli oil and vinegar into a small wok or pan, add the stock and bring to the boil. Reduce the heat to low.

4 Put the Sichuan peppercorns for the garnish into a small pan and dry roast until fragrant, then remove from the heat and crush in a pestle and mortar, or place in a plastic bag and bash with a rolling pin.

5 To serve, either divide the noodles between four bowls or leave in the wok, then ladle on the sauce and top with the stir-fry. Garnish with the Sichuan peppercorns, spring onion and coriander. Drizzle chilli oil over the dish, add a drizzle of sesame oil to taste around the edge of the sauce and serve immediately, with extra chilli oil, if you like.

This is one of Sichuan's most famous dishes and is also served in Chinese restaurants throughout the world. Apparently, it was named after Old Mrs. Chen, who served this in her restaurant. In Sichuan they use Suan miao, thin Chinese leeks, but most cooks substitute spring onions.

The word 'Ma-po' describes Old Mrs. Chen's 'pockmarked complexion'. The Chinese are not known for being very tactful – my grandmother used to refer to a South African friend of mine as 'the one with the "sharp" nose' – she didn't mean it impolitely; to the Chinese, pointed noses are deemed more beautiful. Needless to say, I had some explaining to do to my friend.

'Ma-po' dofu beef

SERVES 4 TO SHARE

300g/11oz minced beef or pork
2 teaspoons Sichuan peppercorns
2 tablespoons groundnut oil
2 garlic cloves, crushed and finely chopped
1 tablespoon freshly grated root ginger
1 red chilli, deseeded and finely sliced
2 tablespoons chilli bean sauce
400g/14oz firm fresh dofu, cut into
  2.5cm/1 inch chunks
200ml/7fl oz hot beef stock
1 teaspoon light soy sauce

1 tablespoon cornflour blended with
  2 tablespoons cold water
2 large spring onions, sliced
sea salt and ground white pepper
steamed jasmine rice (see page 156)
  to serve

FOR THE MARINADE

1 teaspoon toasted sesame oil
1 tablespoon light soy sauce
1 tablespoon Shaohsing rice wine or
  dry sherry

1 Put all the ingredients for the marinade into a bowl and stir to combine. Add the minced meat and leave to marinate for 10 minutes.

2 Heat a wok over a high heat. Add the minced meat and cook until browned, then transfer to a bowl and put to one side.

3 Put the Sichuan peppercorns into a small pan and dry roast until fragrant, then remove from the heat and crush in a pestle and mortar, or place in a plastic bag and bash with a rolling pin. Reheat the wok and add the groundnut oil. Stir-fry half the crushed Sichuan peppercorns to release their aroma, then stir in the garlic, ginger, chilli and chilli bean sauce. Add the minced meat and dofu and stir-fry gently for 2 minutes.

4 Add the hot stock and bring to the boil, then season to taste with the soy sauce, salt and pepper. Add the blended cornflour and stir to thicken. Stir in the spring onions. Sprinkle on the remaining crushed Sichuan peppercorns, and serve with steamed rice.

This is a mouth-tingling numbing hotpot! The spicy soup stock base is a delicious broth in which fresh ingredients are poached – like a Chinese fondue. The Mandarin word for such a feast is 'Huo-guo', meaning firepot, because all the ingredients are cooked in a hotpot!

I love this kind of feast, it is easy to prepare and great for interaction with friends. All you need is an electric wok, set up in the centre of the table, plenty of soup ladles and away you go. I had this dish in Chengdu in the middle of summer and it was fantastic. Be warned – this is extremely spicy.

Spicy hotpot

SERVES 4

FOR THE SPICY SOUP STOCK BASE

2 tablespoons groundnut oil

3–4 long dried Sichuan chillies or long dried chillies

50g/2oz whole Sichuan peppercorns

1 tablespoon chilli bean sauce

1 tablespoon chilli sauce

1.7 litres/3 pints hot vegetable stock

2 star anise

6 dried Chinese mushrooms

1 small handful of dried tangerine peel or zest of 1 orange

250ml/9fl oz chilli oil

2.5cm/1 inch piece of fresh root ginger, peeled

250g/9oz fish balls

250g/9oz fish cake, sliced

2 medium red chillies, deseeded and sliced

1 small handful of Chinese cabbage/leaf, sliced 2.5cm/1 inch thick

1 small handful of deep-fried dofu

1 small handful of fresh dofu, cut into 2.5cm/1 inch chunks

1 large spring onion, roughly chopped

FOR THE POT

1 plate each of:

thin slices of beef, pork fillet and lamb

raw prawns, shelled and deveined

slices of monkfish

fish balls

fresh squid rings

Chinese cabbage/leaf, shredded

dried vermicelli mung bean noodles, pre-soaked in hot water for 5–6 minutes and drained

fresh firm dofu, cut into chunks

enoki mushrooms and baby corn

VINEGAR, CHILLI AND SOY DIPPING SAUCE

To share on the table:
3 tablespoons Chinkiang black rice vinegar or balsamic vinegar
3 tablespoons light soy sauce
1 red chilli, deseeded and finely chopped

SPECIAL TAIWANESE DIPPING SAUCE

To serve 1:
1 egg yolk
1 tablespoon oriental satay/barbeque sauce (see page 184)
1 tablespoon light soy sauce
1 tablespoon finely chopped fresh coriander
1 tablespoon finely sliced spring onion

1 First make the spicy soup stock base. Heat a 2 litre/3½ pint capacity wok over a high heat and add the groundnut oil. Add the chillies and Sichuan peppercorns and stir-fry until fragrant.

2 Add the chilli bean sauce and chilli sauce and then pour in the stock. Add the star anise, dried mushrooms, tangerine peel or orange zest, chilli oil and ginger and bring to the boil, then reduce the heat to low–medium and simmer for 20 minutes.

3 Ten minutes before serving, add the remaining spicy soup stock base ingredients.

4 Whilst the stock is simmering, place all the ingredients for the pot on serving plates, cover with clingfilm and put into the fridge. To make the vinegar, chilli and soy dipping sauce combine all the ingredients and put to one side.

5 To serve, arrange all the ingredients on the table. Transfer the soup base to an electric wok and set it up in the centre of the table. Let guests help themselves and cook the ingredients in the spicy broth. Let each guest prepare their own Taiwanese dipping sauce at the table. Serve with the vinegar, chilli and soy dipping sauce, too.

Ching's tip

Make sure you have plenty of utensils for the raw ingredients at the table and let your guests use those to add anything into the stockpot – this reduces the chance of cross-contamination from the raw ingredients and your guests' serving plates.

For a great vegetarian alternative, leave out the the fish and meat and use more of the vegetables plus vegetarian balls (available from Chinese supermarkets) for the soup stock base, and pak choy and broccoli for the pot.

Sichuan cooking uses a lot of dried tangerine or orange peel in stocks to enhance the flavour of dishes. Inspired by ingredients such as dried tangerine peel and the citrusy-numbing hot Sichuan peppercorns, I have decided to use fresh oranges in my Sichuan orange beef. This dish is oh-so-simple to make and nutritious, too. The flavours are fresh and fruity, and it's one of my favourite healthy midweek suppers.

Sichuan orange beef

SERVES 2

2 beef frying steaks or beef fillet steaks
1 tablespoon groundnut oil
100g/3½oz fresh shiitake mushrooms, sliced
mixed salad leaves or steamed jasmine rice (see page 156) to serve

FOR THE MARINADE

1 tablespoon Shaohsing rice wine or dry sherry
2 tablespoons light soy sauce
2 tablespoons runny honey
4 tablespoons orange juice
1 pinch of freshly ground black pepper

TO GARNISH

1 orange, peeled and segmented
1 spring onion, finely sliced (optional)

1 Put all the ingredients for the marinade into a bowl and stir to combine. Add the beef and leave to marinate for 10–15 minutes.

2 Heat a pan over a high heat and add the groundnut oil. Place the steaks in the pan and cook until browned on one side, then turn over to cook the other side. Cook according to your taste: 1–2 minutes for rare, 2–3 minutes for medium, longer for well done.

3 When the beef is cooked to your taste, add the remaining marinade and cook for a few more seconds. Lift the beef out onto serving plates, cover with foil and keep warm.

4 Add the shiitake mushrooms to the pan and cook until softened.

5 To serve, place the mushrooms alongside the steak and garnish with the orange segments and spring onion, if you like. Serve with mixed salad leaves or steamed jasmine rice.

The name Bang-Bang comes from the word for stick in Mandarin, which is 'Bung'. The chicken meat was beaten with the stick to tenderise it. You could use a rolling pin on cooked chicken breast and then tear the meat into shreds using your fingers.

Bang-Bang chicken

SERVES 2

100g/3½oz dried vermicelli mung bean noodles, pre-soaked in hot water for 5–6 minutes and drained, or use rice noodles

½ cucumber, cut into julienne strips

250g/9oz cooked chicken breast, shredded

50g/2oz radish, sliced

1 large spring onion, finely sliced

1 medium red chilli, deseeded and finely chopped

FOR THE DRESSING

2 tablespoons groundnut oil

1 tablespoon toasted sesame oil

½ teaspoon dried Sichuan chilli flakes or dried chilli flakes

½ teaspoon freshly ground roasted Sichuan peppercorns (see step 1, opposite)

2 tablespoons crunchy peanut butter

1 tablespoon light soy sauce

juice of ½ lemon

1 tablespoon freshly grated root ginger

2 tablespoons water

FOR THE GARNISH

1 teaspoon each toasted black and white sesame seeds or mixed health seeds

1 Arrange the noodles, cucumber, chicken, radish, spring onion and chopped chilli on a plate, cover with clingfilm and chill in the fridge for 20 minutes.

2 Before serving, put all the ingredients for the dressing into a blender and whiz to combine. For a warm dressing, pour from the blender into a small pan and heat for 2 minutes.

3 Pour the dressing over the chicken mixture, sprinkle with the seeds and serve immediately.

The traditional version of this dish uses black rice vinegar for the sourness and sugar for sweetness, but I use lemon juice for the 'sour' and hoisin sauce for a rich sweet flavour. It's great served with white meat or pork shreds, too.

'Gong bao' or 'Kung po' prawns

SERVES 2

FOR THE CRISPY PRAWNS

1 tablespoon whole Sichuan peppercorns
2–3 pinches of sea salt
2 tablespoons cornflour
300g/11oz raw tiger prawns, shelled with
** tail on, deveined**
8 tablespoons groundnut oil

FOR THE STIR-FRY

2 garlic cloves, crushed and finely chopped
1 medium red chilli, deseeded and finely
** chopped**
2 red peppers, deseeded and cut into chunks
1 tablespoon cornflour blended with
** 2 tablespoons cold water**

FOR THE SAUCE

2 tablespoons lemon juice
2 tablespoons hoisin sauce
1 tablespoon dark soy sauce
1 teaspoon crushed dried Sichuan chillies
** or crushed dried chilli flakes**

FOR THE GARNISH AND TO SERVE

1 handful of fresh coriander, leaves and
** stalks, roughly chopped**
1 small handful of dry-roasted peanuts
Beijing rice (see page 156)

1 Put the Sichuan peppercorns into a small pan and dry roast until fragrant, then remove from the heat and crush in a pestle and mortar, or place in a plastic bag and bash with a rolling pin. Put the salt, crushed peppercorns and cornflour into a bowl, add the prawns and turn to coat in the mixture. Heat a wok over a high heat and add the groundnut oil. Add the prawns and stir-fry until they have turned pink and have a crispy coating. Remove from the wok and drain on absorbent kitchen paper.

2 Combine all the ingredients for the sauce and put to one side.

3 Retain 1 tablespoon oil in the wok, reheat and add the garlic and chilli. Stir-fry for less than 1 minute, then add the red peppers and stir-fry for 1 minute. Pour the sauce into the wok and bring to the boil. Add the blended cornflour and stir to thicken the sauce.

4 To serve, place the prawns on a serving plate and pour the hot sauce over them. Garnish with the coriander and peanuts and serve immediately with Beijing rice.

This stir-fry is full of flavour and can be served up in a matter of minutes. The dish was inspired by all the cheap and cheerful seafood places in Hong Kong, where some of the most amazing seafood is served! I was particularly taken with a garlic prawn dish I ate there – the prawns were butterflied (cut in half down the middle of the back), topped with generous amounts of butter, garlic and spring onions and steamed. My zesty chilli and garlic prawns was inspired by that memorable dish. Make sure you buy raw tiger prawns because if you buy cooked, they will be too chewy when cooked again in this dish.

Zesty chilli and garlic tiger prawns

SERVES 2

2 tablespoons groundnut oil

5 garlic cloves, finely chopped

1 medium red chilli, deseeded and finely chopped

200g/7oz raw large tiger prawns, shelled and deveined

1 tablespoon Shaohsing rice wine or dry sherry

juice of 1 lime

75g/3oz French beans, chopped into 1cm/½ inch lengths

1 pinch of sea salt

1 teaspoon dried chilli flakes

1 Heat a wok or pan over a high heat and add the groundnut oil. Add the garlic and chopped chilli and stir-fry for a few seconds, then add the prawns, rice wine or sherry and the lime juice and stir-fry until the prawns start to turn pink.

2 Add the French beans and mix together. When the prawns have all turned pink, season with the salt and chilli flakes and serve immediately.

In Sichuan they love cured pork and for starters you will often find a delicious spicy cucumber salad in vinegar and Sichuan pepper oil. Inspired by these ingredients, I have used smoked bacon or lardons, which gives this dish its smoky saltiness, and Sichuan peppercorns to provide numbing heat. The cucumber and rice vinegar help to cut through those flavours, making this an unbelievably addictive and moreish dish. A great starter, it helps to 'kai-wei' – open up the appetite.

Spicy warm bacon or lardon and cucumber salad

SERVES 2

100g/3½oz smoked lean bacon
    or lardons, or pancetta
1 tablespoon groundnut oil
6 long dried chillies
2 teaspoons Sichuan peppercorns
1 star anise
1 medium red chilli, deseeded
    and finely chopped
1 tablespoon Shaohsing rice
    wine or dry sherry
2 tablespoons toasted sesame oil
2 tablespoons clear rice vinegar
    or cider vinegar
200g/7oz cucumber, halved
    lengthways, deseeded and
    sliced into 1cm/½ inch thick
    wedges
1 pinch of sea salt
1–2 pinches of dried chilli flakes
1 tablespoon lime juice
1 tablespoon chilli oil
1 very small handful of fresh
    coriander leaves, roughly
    chopped
dry-roasted peanuts (optional)

1 Cut the bacon (or lardons) into 1cm/½ inch thick pieces. Heat a wok or pan over a high heat and add the groundnut oil. Add the dried chillies and Sichuan peppercorns and stir-fry for a few seconds until fragrant.

2 Add the star anise and bacon or lardons and stir-fry until they have turned golden brown at the edges. Add the chopped chilli and stir-fry for a few seconds.

3 Add the rice wine or sherry, the sesame oil and vinegar and stir-fry for a few seconds, then add the cucumber and stir-fry for a few seconds.

4 Season with the salt, dried chilli flakes and lime juice.

5 Place on a serving plate, drizzle over the chilli oil, garnish with the chopped coriander, sprinkle over some peanuts, if you like them, and serve immediately.

Ching's tip
If you are vegetarian, substitute chestnut and shiitake mushrooms for the bacon or lardons.

This is a tasty nutritious dish. Here, soya beans that have been made into bean curd are introduced to fresh soya beans (edamame) and the contrast is fabulous – a vegetarian marriage made in culinary heaven. Simple to prepare in a matter of minutes.

Spicy dofu and edamame beans

SERVES 4

FOR THE BEAN CURD STIR-FRY

2 tablespoons groundnut oil
400g/14oz fresh firm bean curd (dofu), drained and cut into rectangles 1cm/½ inch thick
3 tablespoons light soy sauce
1 teaspoon dark soy sauce
1 tablespoon Chinkiang black rice vinegar or balsamic vinegar
1 teaspoon dried chilli flakes
steamed jasmine rice (see page 156) to serve

FOR THE REST OF THE STIR-FRY

1 tablespoon groundnut oil
1 red chilli, deseeded and finely chopped
75g/3oz fresh or frozen edamame beans
1 teaspoon light soy sauce
1 teaspoon Chinkiang black rice vinegar or balsamic vinegar
1 large handful of fresh coriander, leaves and stalks, finely chopped

1 First, make the bean curd stir-fry. Heat the groundnut oil in a large flat-based pan over a medium heat, add the bean curd and cook for 2 minutes. Add the light soy sauce and cook until the sauce has reduced and the bean curd is browned on one side. Using a small palette knife or fork, lift and turn each piece (careful not to break the bean curd) and cook to colour the other side.

2 Add the dark soy sauce and vinegar and cook until the liquid has reduced by half. Season with the dried chilli flakes. Transfer the bean curd to a serving plate and put to one side.

3 Cook the rest of the stir-fry. Heat the pan and add the groundnut oil. Stir-fry the chilli for a few seconds, then add the edamame beans. Add a sprinkle of water to help create steam and cook for less than 1 minute. Season with the light soy sauce and vinegar and then stir in the chopped coriander.

4 To serve, pour the beans over the bean curd or mix together in the pan and serve immediately with steamed rice.

Ching's tip

For meat lovers, add some cut chipolata sausages before you add the beans in step 3. Delicious!

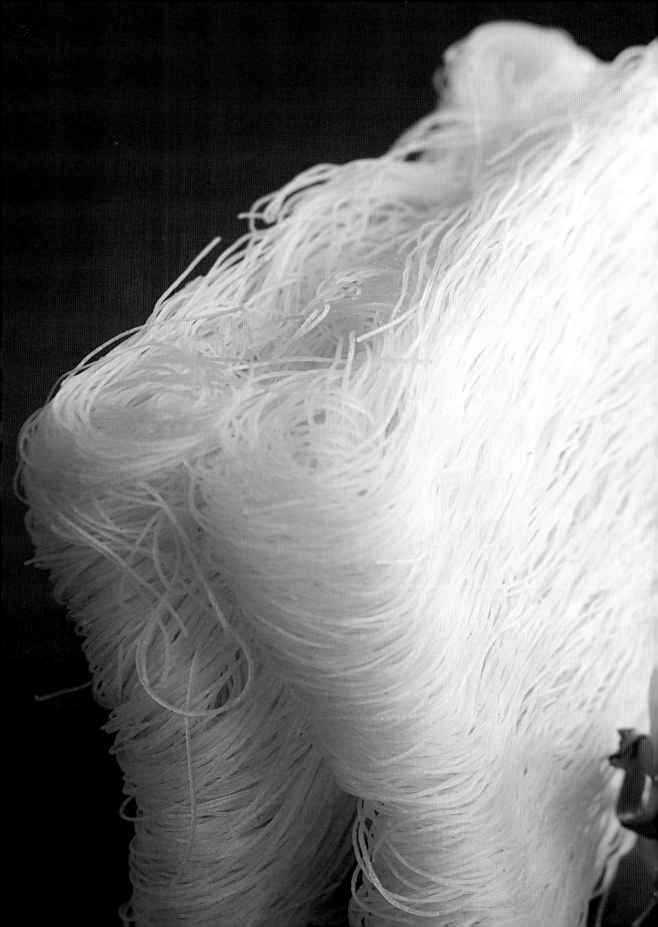

Dumplings, dim sum and noodles

I love this soup; it is earthy from the fragrant Chinese mushrooms and very warming on a cold winter's day. You can adjust the amount of chilli to your taste and omit the chicken strips if you are vegetarian. This is a fast noodle soup – better and more authentic than an instant noodle pot.

Fast hot and sour noodle pot

SERVES 2

1 tablespoon groundnut oil

2.5cm/1 inch piece of fresh root ginger, peeled and finely chopped or grated

1 small handful of fresh shiitake mushrooms, sliced

1 medium red chilli, deseeded and finely chopped

1 tablespoon Shaohsing rice wine or dry sherry

750ml/1¼ pints hot vegetable stock

1 small tin of sliced bamboo shoots, drained

1 tablespoon light soy sauce

1 tablespoon dark soy sauce

1 tablespoon Chinkiang black rice vinegar or balsamic vinegar

1 pinch of ground white pepper

1 tablespoon cornflour blended with 2 tablespoons cold water

300g/11oz cooked egg noodles

2 small handfuls of bean sprouts

60g/2½oz baby corn, sliced

1 spring onion, sliced

100g/3½oz cooked skinless chicken breast fillets, shredded

1 Heat a wok over a high heat and add the groundnut oil. Stir-fry the ginger and mushrooms until softened, then add the chilli, rice wine or sherry, the stock, bamboo shoots and seasonings. Bring to the boil. Add the blended cornflour and stir to thicken the soup, then turn the heat down to very low.

2 Layer the egg noodles, bean sprouts, corn and spring onion in plastic pots or bowls and top with the shredded chicken. Spoon plenty of the soup base over the ingredients, give the noodle pots or bowls a good stir and eat immediately.

My sister-in-law cooked this dish for me one night when we needed a quick midnight snack. However, instead of the gherkin I have used in the recipe below, she used pickled mustard cabbage for the 'sour' kick and spiced it with some chilli, too. These vegetables cannot be bought from Western supermarkets so that's why I've substituted the cornichons or cocktail gherkins for that same briney salty-sour flavour. This is an easy and light meal and one I enjoy again and again.

Sour ginger pork and celery rice noodle soup

SERVES 2

1 tablespoon groundnut oil

250g/9oz pork fillet, thinly sliced

2 tablespoons Shaohsing rice wine or dry sherry

2 tablespoons sliced ginger in white wine vinegar

4 celery stalks, sliced

500ml/18fl oz hot water

60g/2½oz dried vermicelli rice noodles

4 cornichons or cocktail gherkins, sliced

1 tablespoon clear rice vinegar or cider vinegar

1 tablespoon light soy sauce

dash of toasted sesame oil

ground white pepper

1 Heat a wok or pan over a high heat and add the groundnut oil. Add the pork and stir-fry for a few seconds, then, as it starts to turn brown, add 1 tablespoon rice wine or sherry and the ginger.

2 Add the celery and stir-fry for a few seconds until slightly softened.

3 Pour in the hot water, add the noodles and bring to the boil, then add the cornichons or gherkins.

4 Season with the vinegar, the remaining rice wine or sherry, the soy sauce, sesame oil and some pepper. Transfer to a serving dish and serve immediately.

Ching's tip
You can substitute slices of raw chicken breast for the pork, if you prefer, and sliced beef would be just as good, too.

As well as wonton noodle soups, the small fast food restaurants, called Cha Chan Dien, found all over Hong Kong also serve a variety of dishes from roast duck and rice and seafood noodle stir-fries to cuttlefish ball noodle soup. Roast duck noodle soup is also a popular favourite and this is my version. The duck is first marinated to give it extra flavour, the skin is then pan-fried until crispy and the meat is finished off in the oven. Meanwhile, you can be preparing the noodle soup base.

Roast duck noodle soup

SERVES 2

2 duck breast fillets, skin on
fresh coriander sprigs to garnish
  (optional)

FOR THE MARINADE

1 teaspoon five-spice powder
1 tablespoon sesame oil
3 tablespoons hoisin sauce
3 tablespoons soft light brown sugar
  (optional)
3 tablespoons water
1 tablespoon dark soy sauce

FOR THE SOUP BASE

1 litre/1¾ pints chicken stock
2 dried Chinese mushrooms, pre-soaked
  in hot water for 20 minutes, drained

100g/3½oz shredded Chinese
  cabbage/leaf
1 tablespoon light soy sauce
1 tablespoon Shaohsing rice wine or
  dry sherry
1 tablespoon clear rice vinegar or cider
  vinegar
200g/7oz cooked noodles, such as wheat
  flour flat udon noodles
1 spring onion, chopped on the
  diagonal
40g/1½oz bean sprouts
1 large handful of fresh coriander, leaves
  and stalks, roughly chopped
sea salt and freshly ground black
  pepper

For the method, please see overleaf.

1 Place all the ingredients for the marinade in a bowl and stir to combine. Pour into a sealable plastic bag, add the duck, seal the bag and marinate in the fridge for as long as possible – overnight is ideal, but 20 minutes is okay if you don't have much time.

2 Preheat the oven to 200°C/400°F/gas mark 6. Heat a pan over a high heat. Remove the duck from the marinade and pat it dry. Place in the pan, skin side down, and cook for about 1 minute, then turn and cook the other side until golden brown. Transfer to a baking tray, skin side up, and cook in the oven for 15–20 minutes, depending on the size of the duck breast and how well done you like it.

3 Meanwhile, make the soup base. Heat a pan, add the chicken stock and bring to a simmer, then add the Chinese mushrooms and Chinese cabbage and bring to the boil.

4 Stir in the soy sauce, rice wine or sherry and the vinegar, then add the noodles and cook for less than 1 minute. Bring the soup back to the boil, then add the spring onion, bean sprouts and chopped coriander and remove from the heat. Season with salt and pepper.

5 Take the duck breasts out of the oven and leave to rest for a moment, then carve into slices. Ladle some noodle soup into two bowls, place slices of duck on top, garnish with a few coriander sprigs, if you like, and serve.

This is one of my favourite comfort dishes. 'Wonton' (in Cantonese) or 'Hun tun' (in Mandarin Chinese) is served in the Cha Chan Dien fast food restaurants in Hong Kong, and it is so inexpensive that you could have two bowls at one meal. For a fast snack or supper, I make a large batch of the wonton dumplings and then freeze them, separating them in bags, so that I can take out what I need, boil them in some soup stock and voilà! – a nutritious delicious snack or quick dinner is served in a matter of minutes.

'Wonton' noodle soup

SERVES 4

20 wonton wrappers

1 egg, beaten

2 spring onions, sliced, and 1 small handful of fresh coriander to garnish

FOR THE FILLING

250g/9oz minced pork

200g/7oz raw tiger prawns, shelled, deveined and finely chopped

1 large spring onion, finely chopped

1 tablespoon freshly grated root ginger

1 tablespoon light soy sauce

1 tablespoon Shaohsing rice wine or dry sherry

1 teaspoon toasted sesame oil

2 teaspoons cornflour

1 pinch each of sea salt and ground black pepper

FOR THE SOUP BASE

750ml/1¼ pints vegetable stock

½ head Chinese cabbage/leaf, sliced

4 dried Chinese mushrooms

400g/14oz any cooked wheat flour noodles

1 tablespoon light soy sauce

1 tablespoon clear rice vinegar or cider vinegar

1 teaspoon toasted sesame oil

1 Place all the ingredients for the filling into a bowl and mix well.

2 To prevent the wrappers from opening up and separating from the filling once cooked, brush the inside of each wrapper with egg wash. Take one wonton wrapper and place 2 teaspoons of the filling in the centre. Gather up the sides of the wonton wrapper and mould around the filling into a ball shape, twisting the top to secure.

3 Place all the ingredients for the soup base into a large pan and bring to a simmer. Add the wonton dumplings and cook for 5 minutes. Pour the soup and dumplings into a serving bowl, garnish with the spring onions and coriander and serve immediately.

Lobster in Mandarin Chinese is 'Long-xia', which translates as 'dragon prawn'. Dragons to the Chinese are the king of animals (although they are a mythical creature). Here, the translation and name are apt because to me the lobster is the king of prawns.

In Chinese restaurants this dish is called ginger and spring onion lobster noodle. For my version, I love to use yellow bean sauce, which adds a wonderful 'umami' and bouillon stock-like flavour, and coupled with the natural sweetness of the lobster makes this dish really moreish and simply irresistible. This is my ultimate favourite noodle dish.

'Dragon prawn' noodles

SERVES 2

650g/1lb 6oz live lobster
2 tablespoons groundnut oil
5 garlic cloves, crushed
2.5cm/1 inch piece of fresh root ginger, peeled and finely chopped
4 large tablespoons yellow bean sauce
4 tablespoons light soy sauce
2 tablespoons Shaohsing rice wine or dry sherry
350g/12oz cooked yellow shi whole wheat noodles
4 medium spring onions, sliced lengthways

1 Freeze the lobster for 30 minutes. Heat a large pan of boiling water, then very quickly plunge the lobster in the water and cook for about 8 minutes until pink.

2 Lift the lobster out; put the remaining broth to one side. Using a large cleaver or knife, chop off the tail and cut into three sections. Chop off the claws. Divide the body in half lengthways and then spoon out the brown flesh if preferred and discard. Chop each half into two pieces. Using the back of the cleaver, crack the shell of the claws and all the other pieces – this helps to let the sauce the lobster is cooked in seep through and flavour the meat.

3 Heat a wok over a high heat and add the groundnut oil. Add the garlic and ginger and cook for a few seconds. Add the yellow bean sauce, soy sauce and rice wine or sherry and cook for 30 seconds.

4 Add the lobster and stir well to coat the lobster in the sauce. Add the cooked noodles and toss through well. Add 3–4 tablespoons of the liquid the lobster was cooked in (keep the rest to make a good seafood stock). Finally, add the spring onions, toss through well and serve immediately.

This is really two recipes in one – roast pork and pork puffs – and it is another dim sum dish that I absolutely love. Traditionally, to make it extra flaky, chefs would use lard when making the pastry for these roast pork puffs (Char siu so), but I think life's too short to make your own pastry and so, in my version, I have used ready-made bought puff pastry.

Roast pork pastry puffs

MAKES 6

**500g/1lb 2oz or 250g/9oz pork
  fillet (see Ching's tip)**
**225g/8oz ready-made rolled
  puff pastry**
1 egg, beaten
sesame seeds to sprinkle

FOR THE MARINADE

3 garlic cloves, finely chopped
**2 tablespoons finely grated
  fresh root ginger**
4 tablespoons light soy sauce
**2 tablespoons Shaohsing rice
  wine or dry sherry**
2 tablespoons yellow bean sauce
1 tablespoon groundnut oil
2 tablespoons runny honey
**1 pinch each of sea salt and
  ground black pepper**

1 Combine all the ingredients for the marinade in a dish. Add the pork, cover with clingfilm and leave in the fridge to marinate for as long as possible, preferably overnight.

2 When ready to cook, preheat the oven to 180°C/350°F/ gas mark 4. Remove the pork from the marinade and put the marinade to one side. Place the pork in a roasting tin and roast for 20 minutes, then turn it over and roast for a further 20 minutes, basting a few times as the meat cooks. Once cooked, remove from the oven and leave to rest for a few minutes, then cut the pork into dice. (If you are using a 500g/1lb 2oz piece of pork fillet, retain 250g/9oz for another use.) Leave the oven on.

3 Heat the reserved marinade in a pan, add the pork and stir to coat the meat.

4 Cut each sheet of puff pastry into 12 triangles measuring 5cm/2 inches from the top of the triangle to the base. Place a teaspoon of the pork filling in the centre of each triangle, then place another piece of pastry on top and enclose the filling, keeping the triangular shape of the parcel. Press the edges of the triangle together and fold up slightly to give rounded edges. Brush egg wash over the top, place on a roasting tray lined with greaseproof paper and sprinkle sesame seeds over the top of the parcel.

5 Cook in the oven for 15–20 minutes until the pastry is golden. Serve immediately.

Ching's tip
There's enough marinade for 500g/1lb 2oz pork and so you can use the extra Char siu to make roast pork sandwiches, roast pork fried rice or roast pork salad – it's up to you.

Cold noodle salads are called 'Liang-mein', meaning 'cool-noodle'. Many street vendors in China sell the cold noodles in small plastic bags, with shredded carrots, cucumber, bean sprouts, spring onion and chilli, and drizzled with plenty of peanut sauce. The bag is sealed and tossed before being handed to you with a pair of chopsticks so you can start feasting! This is my version.

Peanut chicken noodle salad

SERVES 2

250g/9oz (125g/4oz dried weight) cooked white shi wheat flour noodles
toasted sesame oil
1 tablespoon light soy sauce
2 skinless chicken breast fillets (about 500g/1lb 2oz)
1 large handful of unsalted cashew nuts to garnish

FOR THE PEANUT SAUCE

1 tablespoon groundnut oil
2 small shallots, finely chopped
3 tablespoons crunchy peanut butter
1 medium red chilli, deseeded and finely chopped
6 tablespoons vegetable stock
3 tablespoons water

TO SERVE

1 medium red chilli, deseeded and finely chopped
½ cucumber, halved lengthways, deseeded and finely sliced
1 small handful of bean sprouts
1 small handful of freshly chopped coriander
1 small spring onion, sliced lengthways

1 Toss the noodles in the sesame oil and soy sauce, cover and chill until needed.

2 Boil the chicken until cooked – about 10 minutes, depending on the thickness of the breast. Drain and shred by hand.

3 Dry-fry the cashews for the garnish in a hot pan for a few minutes until browned. Crush in a pestle and mortar, or place in a plastic bag and bash with a rolling pin.

4 To make the peanut sauce, heat a wok over a high heat and add the groundnut oil. Add the shallots and fry for less than 1 minute until translucent, then add the peanut butter and red chilli and stir-fry together for less than 1 minute. Add the stock and water and mix well. As the sauce starts to bubble, turn the heat off and transfer to a bowl. If you like a thick sauce keep as it is, for a thinner sauce add a few tablespoons of water and stir well.

5 Layer the noodles with all the serving ingredients on each plate and then top with the shredded chicken pieces. Finally, drizzle over the warm sauce, sprinkle on the crushed cashew nuts and serve immediately.

Called 'Siu mai', these are open-wrapped steamed pork and prawn dumplings that can be found in all the dim sum restaurants in Hong Kong and across the world. They are sometimes made with a pork and mushroom filling and topped with a red wolfberry (otherwise known as goji berry). However, my favourite has to be with the pork and prawn filling. The prawns are roughly diced so that when they are cooked you can detect a 'bite' from them. This is another of my all-time favourite dim sum snacks and great to serve at a dinner party as a starter with some chilli or soy dipping sauces of your choice.

Pork and prawn dumplings

MAKES 10

10 wonton wrappers
10 goji berries (optional)
groundnut oil to grease
1 tablespoon fiery chilli sauce
2 tablespoons light soy sauce

FOR THE FILLING

125g/4oz minced pork
125g/4oz raw tiger prawns, shelled, deveined and roughly diced
1 large spring onion, finely chopped
1 tablespoon freshly grated root ginger
1 tablespoon light soy sauce
1 tablespoon Shaohsing rice wine or dry sherry
1 teaspoon toasted sesame oil
2 teaspoons cornflour
1 pinch each of sea salt and ground black pepper

1 Mix all the ingredients for the filling in a bowl.

2 Take one wonton wrapper and place 2 teaspoons of the filling in the centre. Then gather up the sides of the wonton wrapper and mould around the filling into a ball shape, leaving the centre exposed (see Ching's tip). Top each dumpling with a goji berry, if you like.

3 Oil the bottom of a bamboo steamer and line with greaseproof paper. Place the dumplings in the steamer, cover with a lid and place over a pan of boiling water (making sure the water does not touch the base of the steamer). Steam the dumplings for 6–8 minutes until cooked.

4 Meanwhile, combine the chilli and soy sauces in a bowl. Serve with the dumplings.

Ching's tip

Pinch the wonton wrapper around the filling firmly to prevent it from opening up and separating from the filling once cooked. To help, brush the inside of each wrapper with egg wash before filling.

In Mandarin Chinese, wheat flour dumplings cooked/boiled in water are called 'Shui-jiao'. 'Shui' means 'water' and 'jiao' means 'edges', because dumplings are folded 'edges' cooked in water. After noodles and buns, dumplings are the most popular dish found in the north of China, where wheat flour is a staple crop. Dumplings can be served steamed, fried, shallow-fried, cooked in soup broth, or boiled and served with a dressing – usually a base of light soy sauce and black rice vinegar. This last method is the one I have chosen for this recipe; it is easy, light, healthy and, above all, tasty!

Pork and mushroom 'water-dumplings'

SERVES 2

12–14 wheat flour dumpling wrappers
1 litre/1¾ pints water

FOR THE FILLING

175g/6oz minced lean pork
50g/2oz shiitake, chestnut or cep mushrooms, very finely diced
50g/2oz celery, very finely diced
2 large spring onions, finely chopped

1 tablespoon Shaohsing rice wine or dry sherry
1 teaspoon toasted sesame oil
1 tablespoon light soy sauce
1 pinch of salt
1 pinch of sugar

FOR THE SOY AND VINEGAR DIPPING SAUCE

3 tablespoons light soy sauce
3 tablespoons Chinkiang black rice vinegar or balsamic vinegar
2 tablespoons toasted sesame oil
1 teaspoon thinly sliced strips of fresh root ginger, 2cm/5 inches in length
1 medium red chilli, deseeded and finely chopped
a few fresh coriander sprigs, finely chopped

1 Combine all the ingredients for the dipping sauce in a small bowl and put to one side.

2 Place all the ingredients for the filling in a bowl and stir well in one direction only to mix.

3 Take a tablespoon of the filling and place in the centre of a wrapper. Dampen the edges of the wrapper with water and fold one corner of the wrapper to the opposite corner to form a triangular parcel. Press to seal the edges. Gather the sealed side of the parcel to form ripples around the edge of the dumpling. Repeat with the rest of the filling and wrappers. Make an extra dumpling for testing later if you like.

4 Heat the water in a wok or pan over high heat until boiling. Gently lower the dumplings into the water and bring to the boil again. Turn down the heat and simmer gently for 5 minutes until the dumplings float to the surface and the dumpling skin has turned from opaque to translucent (or test the extra dumpling to see if it's cooked inside). Turn off the heat.

5 Using a slotted spoon, remove the dumplings from the water, being careful not to break the skin. Place on a serving bowl, spoon some of the dipping sauce over the top and serve the rest separately. Eat immediately!

Ching's tip

You can steam the dumplings, too, or even pan-fry them. If pan-frying, place them in a shallow pan and add a sprinkle of water to create steam to help them cook.

The Chinese name for spring roll is 'Chun-juen', which is a literal translation – 'spring roll', but there is no evidence to suggest they are served only in springtime. Although this dish is served more in Western restaurants than in China, I wanted to include it here as it makes a great starter. In Shanghai's neighbouring province of Zhejiang they serve sweet spring rolls filled with red bean paste – similar to northern China. Spring roll wrappers have to be one of the best inventions – they turn delightfully crispy when fried.

Chicken and vegetable spring rolls

MAKES 6 LARGE OR
12 SMALL SPRING ROLLS

groundnut oil
200g/7oz skinless chicken breast fillets,
 cut into pea-sized pieces
4 dried Chinese mushrooms, pre-soaked
 in hot water for 20 minutes, drained
 and finely chopped
1 tablespoon light soy sauce
1 tablespoon five-spice powder
12 large or 24 small spring roll wrappers,
 thawed if frozen (see Ching's tips)
1 tablespoon cornflour blended with
 1 tablespoon hot water

FOR THE FILLING

1 teaspoon freshly grated root
 ginger
75g/3oz bean sprouts
2 large spring onions, finely sliced
 lengthways
1 small carrot, cut into julienne
 strips

1 tablespoon oyster sauce
½ tablespoon light soy sauce
sea salt and ground white pepper

FOR THE DIPPING SAUCE (OPTIONAL)

25g/1oz dried apricots
2 plums, stoned and cut into slices
½ teaspoon ground allspice
1 teaspoon raisins
1 teaspoon freshly grated root ginger
100ml/3½ fl oz water
1 teaspoon soft light brown sugar
1 teaspoon lime juice
1 pinch of salt

1 To make the dipping sauce, place all the ingredients into a small pan and bring to the boil. Using a stick blender, blend until smooth, then pour into a bowl and leave to cool. Once cooled, it will become thick and jammy and ready to use.

2 Heat a wok over a high heat and pour in 1 tablespoon groundnut oil. Add the chicken and Chinese mushrooms and stir-fry for 1–2 minutes, then season with the soy sauce and five-spice powder. Remove the chicken and mushrooms from the wok and set aside to cool for 10 minutes. Wipe out the wok with absorbent kitchen paper.

3 To make the filling, put the ginger, bean sprouts, spring onions and carrot into a bowl, add the chicken and mushrooms and the oyster sauce, soy sauce and salt and pepper and stir to mix.

4 Take two spring roll wrappers and lay one on top of the other – the extra thickness will prevent the skin from breaking. Spoon 2 tablespoons of filling in the centre of the wrapper. Brush each corner of the wrapper with the blended cornflour. Bring two opposite corners together and, keeping your finger on those edges, bring the bottom corner towards the middle and then roll the pastry with the filling towards the top corner. Tuck the top edge in and seal it with blended cornflour. Continue in the same way until all the wrappers are filled.

5 Heat the wok over a high heat and fill to half its depth with groundnut oil. Heat the oil to 180°C/350°F, or until a cube of bread dropped in turns golden brown in 15 seconds. Deep-fry the spring rolls until golden brown, then remove with a slotted spoon and drain on absorbent kitchen paper. Serve with the dipping sauce, if you like.

Ching's tips

You can substitute duck breast fillet for the chicken, if you like – the method is the same. Serve with the dipping sauce.

For a vegetarian option, omit the chicken and use 200g/7oz soaked dried Chinese mushrooms, or fresh mushrooms, such as chestnut.

Instead of spring roll wrappers, you can use two 12.5 cm/5 inch squares of filo pastry for each wrapper. Brush one sheet with oil, cover with the second sheet and brush with oil again. Fill and roll as in step 4 above, then deep-fry or place on a baking tray and bake at 180°C/350°F/gas mark 4 for 20–25 minutes.

This is another simple and satisfying vegetarian Liang-mein, or cold noodle salad. This dish tastes even better if all the vegetables and noodles are kept chilled before serving. This is the perfect dish to make ahead, especially for a large party.

Radish and sesame soy noodle salad

SERVES 2

200g/7oz cooked whole wheat noodles, drizzled with groundnut oil (see Ching's tip)
200g/7oz radish, washed and quartered
½ cucumber, halved lengthways, deseeded and diced
1 small handful of black sesame seeds or mixed health seeds
fresh coriander sprigs to garnish

FOR THE SESAME SOY DRESSING

3 tablespoons light soy sauce
3 tablespoons toasted sesame oil
3 tablespoons clear rice vinegar or cider vinegar

1 Prepare the noodles, radishes and cucumber and place in the fridge to chill for at least 1 hour.

2 Combine all the ingredients for the dressing in a bowl.

3 To serve, layer the noodles in a large dish with some radish and cucumber and scatter over the seeds. Spoon the dressing over the dish and garnish with coriander sprigs. Serve immediately at the table to share, or you could dish up individual portions, too.

Ching's tip

Instead of noodles, you can use the same quantity of cooked brown rice.

For a colourful topping, chop up 200g/7oz vinegared beetroot and sprinkle on the salad before adding the dressing.

Fish and seafood dishes

Daikon, or white radish, grows abundantly in the Shandong region next to Beijing, also known for its great seafood, and since clams and daikon are plentiful in this part of China, I was inspired to fuse the two ingredients in a recipe.

I love clams and, when coupled with the sweetness of the carrot and daikon, this makes a delicious broth that would be a perfect start to any dinner party. The ginger gives a slight heat and the coriander supplies a gorgeous punch and aroma. If you like meat, try adding pork ribs cut into chunks with the ginger at step 1, and then complete the recipe.

Cleansing clam and daikon soup

SERVES 4

750ml/1¼ pints vegetable stock
2.5cm/1 inch piece of fresh root ginger, peeled and sliced
125g/4oz daikon, peeled and finely sliced
75g/3oz carrot, finely sliced
1 dried Chinese mushroom (optional)
500g/1lb 2oz fresh clams in the shell, well washed
1 large spring onion, sliced lengthways
1 tablespoon Shaohsing rice wine or dry sherry
1 tablespoon toasted sesame oil
1 tablespoon clear rice vinegar or cider vinegar
2–3 pinches each of sea salt and ground white pepper
1 large handful of fresh coriander, leaves and stalks, roughly chopped
fresh coriander sprigs to garnish

1 Pour the vegetable stock into a large pan and bring to the boil. Add the ginger slices, daikon, carrot and Chinese mushroom, if you're using it. Bring back to the boil and cook for 2–3 minutes until the vegetables are tender.

2 Add the clams, spring onion, rice wine or sherry, the sesame oil and vinegar, and season to taste with the salt and pepper.

3 Stir in the chopped coriander, then transfer to one large or four small serving bowls. Garnish with coriander sprigs and serve immediately.

This quick and easy dish needs only a handful of ingredients but is nutritious and tasty. The fragrant garlic chives (jiu cai) impart a garlicky onion flavour. If you can't find them, use baby leeks and spring onions to give the same sort of flavour.

Tiger prawns and garlic chives stir-fry

SERVES 2

1 tablespoon groundnut oil
2 garlic cloves, finely chopped
12 large raw tiger prawns, shelled with tail on, deveined
1 teaspoon Shaohsing rice wine or dry sherry
150g/5oz garlic chives, washed and trimmed to 4cm/1½ inch length pieces, or 150g/5oz cooked marsh samphire (see Ching's tip), woody stems discarded
1 teaspoon light soy sauce
sea salt

1 Heat a wok over a high heat and add the groundnut oil. Add the garlic and stir-fry for a few seconds.

2 Add the prawns and, as they start to turn pink, add the rice wine or sherry.

3 Add the garlic chives or samphire and stir-fry for 1 minute, then season with the soy sauce and salt. Transfer to a serving dish and serve immediately.

Ching's tip

If you like experimenting with your greens and you have a good fishmonger nearby, try marsh samphire. These are small, hardy cactus-looking plants, which can be found along the coast. They're crunchy and delicious – just boil them in unsalted water for 2–3 minutes, drain and then add them to the dish instead of the garlic chives in the final stages of the stir-fry.

My favourite sauce of all time is black bean sauce. I love it cooked in a number of ways, and I think it goes best with shellfish or poultry. This simple low-fat dish is great for a special occasion but make sure it's not for a first date as it contains plenty of garlic!

Black bean steamed scallops

SERVES 2

8 scallops, removed from the shells, de-bearded and coral removed (retain the shells)
175g/6oz (75g/3oz dried weight) dried vermicelli mung bean noodles, pre-soaked in hot water for 5–6 minutes, drained and cut roughly into 10cm/4 inch lengths
chives or spring onions, very finely chopped, to garnish

FOR THE BLACK BEAN PASTE

6 garlic cloves, finely chopped
2.5cm/1 inch piece of fresh root ginger, peeled and finely chopped
1 medium red chilli, deseeded and finely chopped
1 tablespoon fermented salted black beans, washed and crushed into a paste
1 tablespoon Shaohsing rice wine
2 tablespoons light soy sauce
8 teaspoons water

1 Place the cleaned scallops back in their shells. Mix all the ingredients for the black bean paste together in a bowl, or whiz in a blender. Using a small teaspoon, spoon some of the paste on top of each scallop and gently rub in.

2 Wrap some noodles around each scallop, then spoon 1 teaspoon water around the noodles – this helps to keep the noodles moist and adds sauce to the noodles when combined with the steamed juices of the scallops.

3 Divide the scallop shells between two heatproof plates and put each plate into a bamboo steamer, placing one steamer on top of the other. Place the steamers over a pan or wok of boiling water (making sure the water does not touch the base of the steamer) and steam on high heat for 4–5 minutes until the scallops have turned from translucent to opaque. If you do not have a bamboo steamer, place the shells on a large heatproof plate on a rack in a roasting tray. Fill the roasting tray with boiled water from the kettle. Preheat the oven to 180°C/350°F/gas mark 4. Cover the whole roasting tray with foil and place in the oven to steam for 4–5 minutes.

4 Serve the scallops in the bamboo steamers or remove the plates from the oven. Sprinkle some chopped chives or spring onions over the scallop shells and serve immediately.

Fish is traditionally eaten on Chinese New Year because the Mandarin word for fish is 'Yu' and during the festival there is a phrase called 'Nian nian you yu', which translates as 'Every year you have abundance' – whether it's wealth, luck, happiness, good health or all of the above! In addition to the usual 'Gong xi fa cai' (wishing good fortune), this is a popular phrase.

The Chinese serve the fish whole, as it symbolises unity and 'completeness'. When using fillets, the 'incompleteness' can be compensated for by serving uncut whole wheat noodles (uncut noodles symbolise longevity) with a soy, sesame and spring onion sauce to drizzle over the dish.

If you prefer, you can use monkfish, in place of the cod.

Wok-cooked cod with sesame soy sauce

SERVES 2

100g/3½oz dry whole wheat noodles
a few dashes of toasted sesame oil
4 spring onions, sliced into long strips
1 bunch of fresh coriander, roughly
  chopped
3 tablespoons groundnut oil
2 cod fillets (about 320g/11½oz),
  skin on, washed, seasoned with salt
  and pepper

4 garlic cloves, crushed and finely
  chopped
2.5cm/1 inch piece of fresh root ginger,
  peeled and finely chopped
1 medium red chilli, deseeded and
  finely chopped
4–5 tablespoons light soy sauce
2 tablespoons toasted sesame oil

1 Cook the noodles according to the packet instructions, then drain and immediately refresh under cold running water to rinse away the starch and keep them springy. Dress the noodles with sesame oil, toss through half the spring onion strips and a small handful of the chopped coriander and set aside at room temperature.

2 Heat the groundnut oil in a large wok on a high heat. Add the fish to the wok, skin side down, pressing lightly on each of the fillets as it cooks. Cook for 3–4 minutes until the skin is crisp and golden brown. Turn the heat down to medium.

3 Turn the fish over and sprinkle the garlic, ginger and chilli over the fillets. Cook for a further 3–4 minutes (depending on the size of the fillet) until the flesh has turned opaque and flakes when poked with a pair of chopsticks or a fork.

4 Season with the soy sauce and sesame oil and spoon the sauce over the fish. Add the remaining spring onion strips and chopped coriander and cook until the herbs have wilted slightly.

5 To serve, portion some of the dressed noodles on the side of each serving plate. Place a fish fillet, skin side up, on an angle next to the noodles and drizzle some of the wok-fried sesame soy juices over the top. Garnish with the wilted herbs on top and serve immediately.

The salted black beans come from the south of China and if I were ever marooned on a desert island, they are the one ingredient I would miss the most.

For extra flavour put these pungent beans in a jar and fill it with Shaohsing rice wine, so that whenever you need them you can spoon the wine-flavoured beans straight into the wok. Mung bean noodles are a gorgeous noodle as they help to mop up the delicious sauce in this dish – rice noodles do not compare. You can substitute shelled prawns, scallops, chicken or beef for the mussels if you like.

Mussels in black bean sauce with mung bean noodles

SERVES 2

2 tablespoons groundnut oil

3 garlic cloves, finely chopped

1 tablespoon freshly grated root ginger

2 red chillies, deseeded and finely chopped

1 tablespoon fermented salted black beans, rinsed in cold water, drained and mashed with back of a spoon

18 large cooked New Zealand mussels in the shell

150ml/5fl oz hot vegetable stock

1 tablespoon light soy sauce

1 teaspoon dark soy sauce

1 tablespoon cornflour blended with 2 tablespoons cold water

200g/7oz dried vermicelli mung bean noodles, pre-soaked in hot water for 5–6 minutes and drained

2 large spring onions, finely chopped

1 Heat a wok over a high heat and add the groundnut oil. Add the garlic, ginger and chillies and stir-fry for a few seconds, then add the black beans and stir in.

2 Add the mussels and stir-fry for a few seconds, then add the vegetable stock and bring to the boil.

3 Season with the light and dark soy sauce and then add the blended cornflour and stir until the sauce thickens.

4 Add the mung bean noodles and mix well, being careful not to break up the mussels. Cook for 30 seconds, then stir in the spring onions. Transfer to a serving dish and serve immediately.

I love congee in Hong Kong, especially plain congee for breakfast accompanied by salted peanuts, fermented bean curd, pickled cucumber, fried eggs and dried meat 'shavings' – this is the kind of breakfast I was brought up on when I lived with my grandmother in Taiwan. In Hong Kong, my favourite is pork and duck egg congee, served with a fried bread dough stick called 'You tiao' that you use for dunking. There is something very soothing about a good congee; it settles the stomach and to many Chinese a good wholesome bowl is like having chicken soup – the perfect food when you're recovering from the 'flu, when you cannot take anything solid.

Seafood congee

SERVES 2

2 tablespoons groundnut oil

1 tablespoon freshly grated root ginger

2 shallots, finely chopped

3 dried Chinese mushrooms, pre-soaked in hot water for 20 minutes, strained (liquid reserved) and sliced

136g tin bamboo shoots

150g/5oz white-stemmed pak choy, finely chopped

250g/9oz packaged mixed raw seafood, including mussels, squid, prawns, clams (see Ching's tips)

1 tablespoon Shaohsing rice wine or dry sherry

200g/7oz cooked jasmine rice (see page 156)

500ml/18fl oz mushroom stock (soaking liquid from dried Chinese mushrooms) or vegetable stock

2 tablespoons light soy sauce

1 tablespoon toasted sesame oil

2 pinches of ground white pepper

1 handful of fresh coriander, leaves and stalks, finely chopped

1 Heat a wok or pan over a high heat and add the groundnut oil. Add the ginger, shallots and Chinese mushrooms and stir-fry for a few seconds.

2 Add the bamboo shoots, pak choy and raw seafood and mix well. Add the rice wine or sherry and stir to combine.

3 Add the cooked rice and the mushroom soaking liquid or vegetable stock and bring to the boil. Boil for 1 minute.

4 Season with the soy sauce, sesame oil and pepper and mix in the coriander. Transfer to a serving dish and serve immediately.

Ching's tips

If using cooked seafood, add it after the stock at step 3.

For a more authentic congee, you can add overcooked rice – the grains will have broken down more.

Hot sunny days, pool and barbeque parties, and good food – these are the memories this dish evokes for me. When we were living in South Africa my mother used to buy the largest live lobsters one could imagine. She would steam them, scoop out the flesh, and combine it with cooked diced potatoes and carrots, diced cucumber, sliced hardboiled eggs, mayo, salt and pepper, and then stuff the mixture into sweet buns. In the UK I discovered mini brioche buns that take this recipe to another level. Serve these with a chilled glass of bubbly. Enjoy!

Mum's lobster and mayo brioche

MAKES 12

5 large potatoes, peeled, diced and
  boiled
3 large carrots, diced and boiled
3 large eggs, hardboiled and sliced
½ cucumber, halved lengthways,
  deseeded and diced

650g/1lb 6oz lobster, boiled
  (see page 60) and meat shredded
3 tablespoons mayonnaise
a few pinches of salt
a few pinches of cracked black pepper
12 mini brioche buns

1 Place the potatoes, carrots, eggs, cucumber and lobster meat in a large bowl. Add the mayonnaise, season to taste and mix well, then cover and chill for 20 minutes.

2 Before serving, slice the brioche buns horizontally and spoon some lobster mixture into each bun. Slice the bun in half if you like and serve immediately as a luxurious canapé with plenty of chilled bubbly (and don't forget the napkins).

Yum. I first had fried chilli squid in a London restaurant, when I took my first customer there for a meal. It was crunchy, spicy, salty and just delicious served on a bed of sliced iceberg lettuce with plenty of sliced chilli rings. This is my version. It is best to buy fresh squid and prepare it yourself, but if you are pushed for time, you can cheat and buy prepared squid rings, but make sure you buy the raw variety otherwise you risk overcooking them and they will be too chewy.

Fried chilli squid salad

SERVES 2

250g/9oz fresh squid, washed, cleaned
    and sliced into rings (leave any
    tentacles whole)
1 egg, beaten
1 teaspoon sea salt
1 teaspoon crushed dried chilli flakes
$\frac{1}{2}$ teaspoon ground white pepper
6 tablespoons potato flour or cornflour
300ml/10fl oz groundnut oil

FOR THE CHILLI JAM

100ml/3$\frac{1}{2}$fl oz water
2 red chillies, deseeded and finely chopped
5 tablespoons caster sugar

TO SERVE

100g/3$\frac{1}{2}$oz shredded iceberg lettuce
1 carrot, cut into julienne strips
1 large spring onion, sliced lengthways
1 red chilli, deseeded and sliced into rings
1 small handful of freshly chopped
    coriander

1 Put all the ingredients for the chilli jam in a pan and cook for 5 minutes to reduce the liquid by half, then blend the liquid using a blending stick. Pour into a dipping bowl and set aside – as the liquid cools, it will become thick and jammy.

2 Coat the squid rings with the beaten egg. Season with salt, dried chillies and pepper, then dust generously with the flour, coating each ring well.

3 Heat the oil in a wok or pan over a high heat to 180°C/350°F, or until a cube of bread dropped in turns golden brown in 15 seconds.

4 Lower the squid rings into the oil and fry until golden brown, then remove from the pan and drain on absorbent kitchen paper.

5 Place the squid on a bed of shredded lettuce and carrot strips and sprinkle with generous amounts of spring onion, chillies and coriander. Serve with the chilli jam.

In Shanghai's neighbouring region of Jiangsu, river fish and river prawns, as well as poultry, are cooked in vinegar. In this recipe, I have chosen to use scallops, which are widely available in Shanghai, coupled with some roasted ham. The result is a gorgeous smoky, sweet dish that is so fragrant and cooks in less than a minute. This is a great dinner party dish that can be served together with a number of other dishes. Don't underestimate it — as well as being really easy, it is also delicious with a capital D!

Chinkiang vinegar scallops with ham

SERVES 2

175g/6oz raw scallops on the shell
2 tablespoons groundnut oil
1 tablespoon freshly grated root ginger
60g/2½oz diced cooked roasted ham or diced unsmoked lardons
1 tablespoon Shaohsing rice wine or dry sherry
1 tablespoon Chinkiang black rice vinegar or balsamic vinegar
½ tablespoon light soy sauce
1 small handful of fresh coriander, leaves and stalks, finely chopped
mixed exotic salad leaves, such as mizuna and red chard, to serve (optional)

1 Remove the scallops from their shells, then remove and discard the hard muscle on the side. Leave the coral on, if you like, or remove it. Trim and rinse the scallops and pat dry.

2 Heat a wok or pan over a high heat and add the groundnut oil. Add the ginger and stir-fry for a few seconds.

3 Add the scallops and ham or lardons and stir-fry for 30 seconds. Add the rice wine or sherry, the vinegar and soy sauce and cook for 1 minute to reduce the sauce. The scallops will turn opaque as they cook.

4 Once the scallops are cooked, add the coriander and mix well. Turn out into a serving dish and serve immediately with some mixed salad leaves, if you like.

This dish was inspired by my visit to the beautiful West Lake in Hangzhou, about two hours away from Shanghai. There I came across the most fragrant and delicious tea – Longjing. In my recipe, the tea leaves are fried until crunchy and crisp – almost like crispy seaweed – and are then sprinkled on top of the prawns. You can use any green tea leaves, but Longjing are milder than most.

Coriander prawns and Longjing tea

SERVES 2

1 egg
100g/3½oz potato flour
groundnut oil
8 large raw tiger prawns,
shelled with head off, tail on,
and deveined
steamed jasmine rice (see page
156) to serve

FOR THE HERBY SAUCE

2 garlic cloves, crushed
1 medium green chilli, deseeded
and roughly chopped
1 large handful of fresh
coriander, leaves and stalks
4 large broccoli florets
2 pinches of sea salt
1 tablespoon Longjing tea leaves
or other green tea leaves

FOR THE CRISPY TEA LEAVES

1 tablespoon groundnut oil
2 tablespoons Longjing tea
leaves or other green tea
leaves

1 Put the egg and potato flour into a bowl and mix well to form a batter.

2 Heat a wok or pan over a high heat and fill to a quarter of its depth with groundnut oil. Heat the oil to 180°C/350°F, or until a cube of bread dropped in turns golden brown in 15 seconds.

3 Dip the prawns in the batter one by one and lower them into the oil. Cook the prawns until they turn golden, then remove from the oil and drain on absorbent kitchen paper.

4 Place all the ingredients for the herby sauce in a container suitable for use with a hand stick blender and blend well.

5 Drain the wok of oil, wipe clean with absorbent kitchen paper and return the wok to the heat. Add the sauce and bring to the bubble, then take off the heat.

6 To make the crispy tea leaves, heat the groundnut oil in a small pan over a high heat, add the tea leaves and lightly fry until they are crisp. Remove from the pan and drain on absorbent kitchen paper.

7 Place the prawns on a serving plate, pour the hot sauce over them, sprinkle with the crispy tea leaves and serve immediately with steamed rice. Alternatively, serve the sauce as a dipping sauce for the prawns.

After a visit to Shanghai, I had an obsession with crabs and, inspired by my trip, I invented this dish. It is not quite a traditional recipe and you may be surprised by the use of ketchup, but it provides a delicious sweetness, which complements the spicy kick. Enjoy! You can serve this recipe as a starter without the noodles. I like to serve this dish with homemade ginger juice to drink.

Chilli crabs with ginger 'juice'

SERVES 2

4 tablespoons groundnut oil

6 large garlic cloves, finely chopped

2 tablespoons freshly grated root ginger

3 medium red chillies, deseeded and finely chopped

300g/11oz small live crabs, killed (see page 60), washed and chopped in half , or fresh, ready-cooked crabs

150ml/5fl oz water

1 tablespoon fresh lime juice

300g/11oz fine egg noodles, cooked and drained

1 spring onion, sliced lengthways, and 1 large handful of fresh coriander, leaves and stalks, roughly chopped, to garnish

FOR THE CHILLI CRAB SAUCE

250ml/9fl oz water

5 tablespoons tomato ketchup

2 tablespoons light soy sauce

1 tablespoon sugar

2 teaspoons cornflour

FOR THE GINGER 'JUICE' (OPTIONAL)

500ml/18fl oz water

2cm/³/₄ inch piece of fresh root ginger, peeled and sliced

3 x 3cm/1¹/₄ inch pieces of rock sugar or 2–3 tablespoons soft light brown sugar

1 Put all the ingredients for the chilli crab sauce into a bowl and mix well. Put to one side.

2 To cook the crabs, heat a wok over a high heat and add the groundnut oil. Add the garlic, ginger and chillies and stir-fry for 30 seconds. Add the crabs to the wok and stir-fry for a further 3–4 minutes until the crab turns red in colour (for freshly killed crab), or 1–2 minutes for ready-cooked crab. Stir in the chilli crab sauce and cook for 1 minute, then add the water and lime juice. Add the noodles and mix well, then top with spring onion slices and chopped coriander and serve immediately.

3 To make the ginger 'juice', heat the water in a small pan, add the ginger pieces and bring to the boil. Add the sugar to taste and simmer on a low heat for 5 minutes before serving.

street food

This is one of my favourite street food dishes. In Taiwan they sell this dish in night markets served in newspapers and sprinkled with pickled spicy daikon (white turnip salad).

I love serving this as a starter or a lunch for friends. You can prepare most of the ingredients in advance and then fry the duck just before serving.

Crispy fragrant duck

SERVES 2

2 duck legs (about 600g/1lb 5oz in
    total), skin on
75g/3oz potato flour or cornflour
groundnut oil for deep-frying
1 pinch of salt
1 pinch of crushed dried chillies

FOR THE MARINADE

½ teaspoon ground cinnamon
½ teaspoon ground ginger
½ teaspoon ground allspice
2 tablespoons Shaohsing rice wine
    or dry sherry
2 tablespoons runny honey
1 tablespoon chilli sauce
1 tablespoon light soy sauce
2 garlic cloves, minced

FOR THE PICKLED RADISH SALAD

100g/3½oz radish, finely diced
½ cucumber, halved lengthways,
    deseeded and finely diced
1 medium red chilli, deseeded and
    finely chopped (optional)
1 tablespoon clear rice vinegar or
    cider vinegar
½ teaspoon salt
1 teaspoon caster sugar
½ teaspoon Shaohsing rice wine
    or dry sherry
1 small handful of fresh coriander
    leaves, finely chopped

1　Place the duck legs in a bowl or sealable plastic bag together with all the marinade ingredients. Cover with clingfilm or seal the bag and leave in the fridge to marinate for as long as possible, preferably overnight.

2　Place all the ingredients for the pickled radish salad in a bowl and combine well. Cover and set aside in the fridge for 1 hour.

3　Heat the oven to 180°C/350°F/gas mark 4. Place the duck legs, rounded side up, in a roasting tin and roast for 10 minutes, then turn the oven up to 220°C/425°F/gas mark 7 for 5 minutes to cook the meat to well done. Remove from the oven and set aside for 2 minutes to cool slightly.

4　Slice the duck into bite-sized slices, dust the slices in the flour and coat well.

5　Heat a wok or pan over a high heat and fill to a quarter of its depth with groundnut oil. Heat the oil to 180°C/350°F, or until a cube of bread dropped in turns golden brown in 15 seconds. Place the duck pieces in a spider/scoop, lower into the oil and fry until crispy and golden brown. Remove from the pan and drain on absorbent kitchen paper.

6　To serve, spoon some pickled radish salad onto each plate and spoon some of the crispy duck slices on top. Sprinkle a pinch of salt and some dried chilli flakes over the duck pieces and serve immediately.

Street stalls in China, Hong Kong and Taiwan sell stinky fried dofu (the dofu is fermented to create the 'stink') called 'tso-dofu', which is usually doused in chilli sauce and served with pickled spicy cabbage – delicious. Every time I make dofu – whether it's a salad or a stir-fried dish – it reminds me of those stalls. Don't worry, this dofu recipe is healthy, light and not smelly at all!

Fast dofu salad

SERVES 2

400g/14oz fresh silken dofu (bean curd), sliced into 2.5 x 2.5cm/1 x 1 inch chunks
100g/3½oz baby spinach leaves, shredded
50g/2oz bean sprouts (optional)
1 red pepper, deseeded and sliced
2 tablespoons olive oil, plus extra for drizzling
1 red onion, sliced
1–2 pinches of soft light brown sugar
pumpkin health seed mix, lightly dried
1 small pinch each of mustard and cress and purple radish seedlings
sea salt and ground black pepper

FOR THE DRESSING

2 tablespoons olive oil
2 tablespoons light soy sauce
2 tablespoons orange juice
2 tablespoons balsamic vinegar
1 red chilli, deseeded and finely chopped
1 pinch of black pepper

1 Place all the ingredients for the dressing in a bowl and whisk to combine. Set aside.

2 Layer the dofu, spinach leaves and bean sprouts, if you like (they give extra crunch), on two serving plates. Cover and place in the fridge to chill.

3 Heat the oven to 200°C/400°F/gas mark 6. Place the red pepper slices on a baking tray, drizzle with olive oil, season with salt and pepper and toss to mix well. Roast for 4–5 minutes until browned and softened. Turn off the oven.

4 Heat a wok over a high heat and add 2 tablespoons olive oil. Add the red onion and cook for 2–3 minutes until softened, then add the brown sugar and cook until the onion is caramelised. Set aside.

5 To serve, sprinkle some of the roasted sweet peppers and caramelised onions around the dofu salad on each plate. Pour some of the dressing over the top, sprinkle with dried pumpkin seed mix and cress and serve immediately.

This is a dish from the south of China. The eggs are hardboiled and then the shell is lightly cracked all over using the back of a teaspoon. They are then re-boiled in a black tea broth infused with delicious seasonings such as star anise and soy. The seasoned liquid makes its way between the cracks and dyes the surface of the boiled egg, giving a marbled effect, while the seasonings impart their flavours into the egg. The longer you leave the eggs to steep in the liquid, the more prominent the marbled effect. They make delicious snacks and can be eaten hot or cold, but I love serving them as a cold starter.

Marbled tea eggs with oyster sauce

SERVES 4

10 hardboiled eggs, shell lightly cracked all over
½ of the reserved broth from Five-spice beef and sesame dressing (see page 110)
2 black tea bags

TO SERVE

2 tablespoons oyster sauce
1 large spring onion, finely sliced
1 small handful of fresh coriander, leaves and stalks, roughly chopped

1 Place the eggs in the broth, add the tea bags and cook on a low heat for 1 hour. Take off the heat and leave the eggs in the liquid until cooled, then cover and refrigerate until needed.

2 To serve, remove the eggs from the liquid and peel to reveal their marbled effect. Slice, drizzle generously with the oyster sauce and garnish with the spring onion and coriander.

These delicious parcels are great as a starter, or served as a main course to share. Meat lovers can add a few thinly sliced slivers of chicken or pork after the garlic and ginger, or cut 100g/3½oz honey roast ham slices into pieces and add after you've seasoned the stir-fry in step 4. Instead of garlic chives, add chopped garlic and use sliced baby corn and spring onions to provide texture and flavour. For children, omit the garlic and garlic chives and add some chopped sweet peppers.

Stir-fried vegetable pancakes

SERVES 4

**2 tablespoons groundnut oil,
  plus extra to grease**
12 small wheat flour pancakes
3 eggs, lightly beaten

FOR THE VEGETABLE
STIR-FRY FILLING

1 tablespoon groundnut oil
2 garlic cloves, finely chopped
**1 tablespoon freshly grated
  root ginger**
125g/4oz bean sprouts
125g/4oz garlic chives
1 tablespoon light soy sauce
dash of toasted sesame oil
**1 pinch of ground white
  pepper**

FOR THE GARNISH

**1 tablespoon pickled red
  cabbage in vinegar**
**1 small handful of roasted
  soya beans, crushed**

1 Oil the base of a small bamboo steamer and place the pancakes inside. Place over a small pan of boiling water (making sure the water does not touch the base of the steamer), cover and steam for 5–6 minutes. Take off the heat and keep warm, covered in the steamer until ready to serve.

2 Heat a wok over a high heat and add 2 tablespoons groundnut oil. Add the beaten eggs and scramble, then put to one side.

3 Make the stir-fry filling. Return the wok to the heat and add the groundnut oil, followed by the garlic and ginger, and stir-fry quickly for a few seconds to release the aroma. (Add thinly sliced meat, if you prefer, at this stage and cook for 1 minute.)

4 Add the bean sprouts and garlic chives and cook until the vegetables are tender but still with a bite. Return the scrambled eggs to the wok and season with the soy sauce, sesame oil and pepper. Transfer to a large plate and garnish with the pickled red cabbage and crushed soya beans.

5 To serve, place the plate in the centre of the table together with the pancakes in the steamer. To eat, fold a pancake in half and then in half again to give a fanned conical shape (see left), stuff the pancake with the vegetable filling and eat immediately.

If you are a fan of sweet and sour, this is a delicious, fruity stir-fry that will have you craving for more. It makes a very quick supper. Vary the quantity of mango to your taste. Use fresh mangoes if possible.

Mango chicken

SERVES 2

2 tablespoons groundnut oil

1 tablespoon freshly grated root ginger

100g/3½oz skinless chicken breast fillets, cut into thin slices

1 tablespoon Shaohsing rice wine or dry sherry

1 green chilli, deseeded and finely chopped

1 red pepper, deseeded and cut into 2.5 x 2.5cm/1 x 1 inch chunks

200ml/7fl oz puréed mangoes (1 large mango, peeled, stoned, sliced and blended)

150ml/5fl oz pineapple juice, or, if using tinned mangoes, syrup from the tin

1 tablespoon light soy sauce

1 pinch of ground black pepper

½ fresh mango, peeled, stoned and sliced

steamed jasmine rice (see page 156) to serve

1 Heat a wok or pan over a high heat and add the groundnut oil. Add the ginger and stir-fry for a second or two, then add the chicken breast and mix well. Add the rice wine or sherry as the chicken starts to cook, stirring all the time to make sure the ginger does not catch and burn.

2 Add the chilli and red pepper and stir-fry for 1 minute.

3 Add the mango purée and the juice and season the dish with the soy sauce and pepper. Let the liquid bubble and reduce for 1 minute.

4 Finally, add the fresh mango slices and stir-fry for 30 seconds. Transfer to a serving dish and serve immediately with steamed rice.

In Hong Kong they love, and are famed for their skill at, rôtisserie-style cooking, where whole ducks, chickens and pigs, with their entrails, are roasted to a golden or soy colour. Inspired by this style of cooking, my simple five-spice roast drumsticks make a simple dinner.

Five-spice roast chicken drumsticks

SERVES 4

1kg/2¼lb chicken drumsticks, skin on
steamed jasmine rice (see page 156) and orange fennel salad (see page 107) to serve

FOR THE MARINADE

1 tablespoon groundnut oil
3 garlic cloves, crushed and chopped
2 tablespoons freshly grated root ginger
1 tablespoon Shaohsing rice wine or dry sherry
2 tablespoons light soy sauce
2 teaspoons five-spice powder
2 tablespoons runny honey

1 Place all the ingredients for the marinade into a large bowl and stir to combine. Add the chicken and cover the bowl with clingfilm, then place in the fridge and marinate for as long as possible – overnight is ideal, but 10 minutes is okay if you don't have much time.

2 When ready to cook, preheat the oven to 180°C/ 350°F/gas mark 4. Place the chicken on a roasting tray and roast for 30 minutes until the skin is golden. Serve with steamed rice and orange fennel salad.

In Beijing there are many street stalls selling Muslim delicacies and snacks such as Chuan rou (in Mandarin Chinese, 'Chuan' means 'skewered' and 'rou' means 'meat') – in fact, they have become so popular they are found all over China, and not just in the north.

Here, the meat is coated in spices, skewered, and then cooked on a grill or barbeque, which gives it an irresistible smoky flavour. I like it served with a simple orange fennel salad, which complements the spiciness of the dish.

Spiced skewered lamb

SERVES 2

200g/7oz lamb fillet, very finely sliced and then cut into small pieces
olive oil

FOR THE SEASONING

1 teaspoon ground cumin
1 teaspoon fennel seeds
1 teaspoon dried chilli flakes
½ teaspoon paprika
½ teaspoon sea salt
1 teaspoon light soy sauce
1 teaspoon groundnut oil

1 teaspoon Shaohsing rice wine or dry sherry

FOR THE ORANGE FENNEL SALAD

4 tablespoons olive oil
3 tablespoons orange juice
juice of ½ lime
1 tablespoon light soy sauce
1 teaspoon toasted sesame oil
200g/7oz mixed washed salad leaves
1 fennel, finely sliced, soaked in cold water for 30 seconds, then drained
2 oranges, peeled and segmented
sea salt and ground black pepper

1   Soak 8–10 wooden skewers in water for about 20 minutes.

2   Combine all the ingredients for the seasoning in a bowl. Add the meat and stir to coat in the spices, then thread the meat onto the skewers.

3   Heat a griddle pan over a high heat and add a drizzle of olive oil. Place the skewers in the pan and cook until browned on one side, then turn them over and cook for l minute. Take off the heat.

4   To make the dressing for the salad, put the olive oil, orange juice, lime juice, soy sauce, sesame oil, salt and pepper into a bowl and mix well. Put the salad leaves into another bowl and top with the fennel, then add the orange segments and drizzle the dressing over the salad.

5   To serve, divide the salad between two plates and then place the skewers of lamb on top.

This is a famous Taiwanese street-hawker snack. I had to do some serious bribing for this recipe when I watched a chef make this dish. Here is my adapted version – I use chicken thighs, as the meat is a lot juicier than breast, but drumsticks would work just as well. I like to serve this dish on some crisp romaine lettuce leaves, shredded carrots and tomatoes or a simple leaf salad (both are healthy options) or you could accompany it with some steamed rice or chunky chips and some ice cold beer. Enjoy!

Crispy chicken

SERVES 2

350g/12oz chicken thighs, each chopped in half across the bone

7 tablespoons potato flour or cornflour

groundnut oil

1 medium red chilli, deseeded and finely chopped

½ spring onion, green part only, finely chopped

mixed leaf salad to serve

FOR THE MARINADE

2 garlic cloves, minced

2 tablespoons light soy sauce

½ tablespoon salt

½ tablespoon five-spice powder

1 teaspoon toasted sesame oil

1 Mix all the ingredients for the marinade in a bowl and add the chicken pieces, turning to coat. Cover with clingfilm and leave in the fridge to marinate for as long as possible, preferably overnight.

2 Remove the chicken from the marinade and coat in the flour.

3 Heat a wok or pan over a high heat and fill to half its depth with groundnut oil. Heat the oil to 180°C/350°F, or until a cube of bread dropped in turns golden brown in 15 seconds. Add the chicken and fry lightly on medium heat for 6–8 minutes (depending on the size of the chicken pieces) until golden brown on all sides. Remove from the pan and drain on absorbent kitchen paper.

4 Sprinkle with the chopped chilli and spring onion and serve immediately, accompanied by a mixed leaf salad.

Ching's tip

To whet the appetite before enjoying this chicken and to get any street party going, slice some plum tomatoes in half, stuff each one with salted dried plums and place in a small bowl. In Taiwan, street sellers serve these in small bags ready to take away with you. They also grind the dried salted plums and sprinkle over fruit for a punchy tangy bite.

This American-Chinese dish is very popular in American takeaways and Chinese fast food outlets. It is basically a folded omelette with plenty of Chinese ingredients such as bean sprouts, water chestnuts, dried shrimps, mushrooms, roast pork and shredded chicken, served with a soy sauce 'gravy'. I like mine filled with plenty of shiitake mushrooms, diced bacon, red pepper and spring onions, served with salad, some red pepper and sweet chilli sauce, and washed down with orange juice – the perfect summer brunch.

Egg fu young

SERVES 2 GENEROUSLY
groundnut oil
1 small handful of shiitake mushrooms or chestnut mushrooms, sliced
1 red pepper, deseeded and diced
75g/3oz smoked bacon, diced
5 eggs, lightly beaten
a dash of light soy sauce
1 pinch of ground black pepper

TO SERVE
mixed salad leaves
red pepper and sweet chilli sauce (see page 169) or tabasco sauce

1 Heat a wok over a high heat and add 1 tablespoon groundnut oil. Add the mushrooms, red pepper and bacon and stir-fry for 1 minute until fragrant.

2 Add the stir-fry mixture to the eggs, discarding any liquid from the wok. Season with soy sauce and black pepper.

3 Wipe out the wok, heat over a high heat and add 2 tablespoons groundnut oil, swirling to coat the wok. Add half the beaten egg mixture and cook for 1 minute until slightly brown on the underside, then flip over and cook for another minute on the other side. Place on a warmed plate and cover with foil whilst you make the second omelette in the same way.

4 Serve the omelette with mixed salad leaves and red pepper and sweet chilli sauce, or even a few drops of tabasco sauce.

This is my alternative to roast beef. The beef cooking liquid can be used to create another recipe – delicious marbled tea eggs, a street snack found in the south of China. These eggs when cooled and sliced can be served as an accompaniment to this dish, or eaten on their own as a snack. To make the marbled tea eggs, see page 101.

Five-spice beef and sesame dressing

SERVES 4

FOR THE CASSEROLE

500g/1lb 2oz stewing or braising
   beef
2 large spring onions, chopped
5cm/2 inch piece of fresh root ginger,
   peeled and sliced
3 tablespoons clear rice wine or
   cider vinegar
1 tablespoon five-spice powder
1.4 litres/2½ pints hot beef stock
3 tablespoons light soy sauce
2 tablespoons dark soy sauce
1 teaspoon sea salt
2 tablespoons soft dark brown sugar

FOR THE SPICY SESAME OIL DRESSING

1 tablespoon sesame paste or tahini paste
juice of ½ lemon
1 garlic clove, crushed
1 tablespoon water
1 tablespoon groundnut oil
1 tablespoon light soy sauce
½ teaspoon chilli flakes

FOR THE GARNISH

1 large spring onion, finely sliced
1 medium red chilli, deseeded and sliced
1 small handful of fresh coriander, leaves
   and stalks, finely chopped
toasted black and white sesame seeds or
   mixed health seeds
chilli oil
1 tablespoon Sichuan peppercorns

1 Place all the ingredients for the casserole into a casserole dish, cover and cook over a medium heat for 45 minutes. Lift the beef out of the dish and leave to cool. Reserve the cooking juices, if you like, for making marbled tea eggs (see page 101). Once the beef has cooled, slice along the grain. Put the slices on a plate, cover and refrigerate for about 15 minutes.

2 When ready to serve, put all the ingredients for the dressing into a blender and blitz to combine. Drizzle over the beef, garnish with the spring onion, chilli and coriander and sprinkle on the toasted seeds. Add a drizzle of chilli oil. Put the Sichuan peppercorns into a small pan and dry roast until fragrant, then remove from the heat and crush in a pestle and mortar, or place in a plastic bag and bash with a rolling pin. Sprinkle over the dish and serve immediately.

There is a large population of Muslim Chinese in Beijing. They came from western China and brought with them a unique cuisine that calls for the use of spices such as cumin and fennel, which found their way to China along the Silk Route. Lamb and mutton are the preferred choice of meat of the Muslim Chinese, but you can use any red meat. The spices in the dish are distinct and extremely flavourful, but the crème de la crème is the addition of lots of chopped spring onion and coriander to complement the meat. Who said that tasty dishes need be complicated?

Spiced beef stir-fry topped with spring onion and coriander

SERVES 2

400g/14oz fillet of beef
2 tablespoons groundnut oil
1 teaspoon Shaohsing rice wine or dry sherry
1 tablespoon light soy sauce
1 pinch of sea salt
1 large handful of fresh coriander, leaves and stalks, roughly chopped
1 spring onion, finely chopped

FOR THE SPICY COATING

2 tablespoons freshly ground cumin
2 tablespoons dried chilli flakes
1 teaspoon ground black pepper
½ teaspoon sea salt

1 Prepare the fillet of beef by hammering it with a meat cleaver or the side of a Chinese cleaver. Slice into wafer-thin slices.

2 Mix all the ingredients for the spicy coating on a plate. Coat the beef in the spice mix.

3 Heat a wok or pan over a high heat and add the groundnut oil. Add the beef and stir-fry for less than 1 minute until browned and tender. As the beef starts to cook, add the rice wine or sherry and season with the soy sauce and a pinch of salt. Take off the heat, stir in the coriander and spring onion and serve immediately.

Ching's tip
You can also serve this on steamed thin wheat flour pancakes, stuffed into warmed flatbreads or warmed wheatflour tortilla wraps, and topped with plenty of wasabi mayo (see page 169).

Celebration food for
family and friends

This dish originates from the north of China, and was originally a stir-fried dish of finely chopped pork and Chinese cabbage served stuffed in soft steamed wheat flour buns. This is my modern version – yum!

Mu shu chicken

SERVES 4

4 tablespoons groundnut oil

2 eggs, lightly beaten

1 garlic clove, crushed and finely chopped

1 tablespoon freshly grated root ginger

250g/9oz skinless chicken breast fillets, diced

1 tablespoon Shaohsing rice wine or dry sherry

2 dried Chinese mushrooms, pre-soaked in hot water for 20 minutes, drained and finely diced

1 small carrot, diced

50g/2oz preserved mustard greens or gherkins, finely diced, or courgettes

50g/2oz dried wood ear mushrooms, pre-soaked in hot water for 20 minutes, drained and finely chopped, or diced fresh shiitake or chestnut mushrooms

120g tin bamboo shoots, drained and diced

1 handful of dry-roasted peanuts

2 tablespoons light soy sauce

1 teaspoon toasted sesame oil

2–3 pinches of ground white pepper

TO SERVE

12 small wheat flour pancakes, steamed in a bamboo steamer for 5–6 minutes or 12 leaves from a small iceberg lettuce

1 Heat a wok over a high heat and add 2 tablespoons groundnut oil. Add the eggs and cook until scrambled. Remove from the wok and put to one side. Wipe the wok clean.

2 Heat the wok and add the remaining groundnut oil. Stir-fry the garlic and ginger for a few seconds, then add the chicken and cook for 1 minute until it starts to turn slightly brown. Add the rice wine or sherry and stir well. Stir-fry for a few seconds, then add the dried Chinese mushrooms and carrot and stir-fry for 1 minute.

3 Add the mustard greens, gherkins or courgettes, the dried or fresh mushrooms, the bamboo shoots and peanuts and mix well. Stir in the scrambled eggs. Season with the soy sauce, sesame oil and pepper and transfer to a serving dish.

4 To serve, place the dish in the centre of the table together with the pancakes in the steamer or the lettuce leaves. To eat, fold a pancake in half and then in half again to give a fanned conical shape, stuff the pancake with the chicken filling and eat immediately. Alternatively, stuff each lettuce leaf with the filling.

This is a simple stir-fry that is quick to make, healthy and delicious. I have used tinned bamboo shoots, but I'm still hoping that fresh bamboo will make it onto the supermarket shelves one day. I'm all for supporting and using local produce, but sometimes it's good to get the exotic stuff, too.

Chicken and bamboo shoot stir-fry

SERVES 2

1 tablespoon groundnut oil

2 garlic cloves, finely chopped

3 dried Chinese mushrooms, pre-soaked in hot water for 20 minutes, drained and chopped

225g/8oz skinless chicken breast fillets, cut into thin strips

1 teaspoon Shaohsing rice wine or dry sherry

1 tablespoon light soy sauce

1 teaspoon dark soy sauce

a few pinches of five-spice powder

100g/3½oz pickled chilli bamboo shoots, drained and cut into strips

1 cucumber, peeled and sliced lengthways using a potato peeler, slices deseeded

steamed jasmine rice (see page 156) to serve

1 Heat a wok over a high heat and add the groundnut oil. Add the garlic and mushrooms and stir-fry for a few seconds.

2 Add the chicken breast and, as the meat starts to cook, add the rice wine or sherry and stir-fry for 1 minute.

3 Season with the light and dark soy sauce and the five-spice powder and stir well.

4 Add the bamboo shoots and cucumber slices and stir well. Serve with steamed rice.

Ching's tip

Fresh bamboo shoots are also good just boiled and served cold as a salad with mayonnaise — something my grandmother used to make as an appetiser. However, fresh bamboo (if you can find it) is time-consuming to prepare — tough fibrous leaves have to be removed and the shoots inside boiled for a long time to make them tender.

This is the perfect make-ahead dish when you have guests coming – it is served cold and the longer you soak the chicken in the dressing, the more delicious it becomes.

Drunken chicken

SERVES 2

450g/1lb chicken thighs, skin on

2.5cm/1 inch piece of fresh root ginger, peeled and sliced

1 large spring onion, chopped into 7.5cm/3 inch lengths

1 teaspoon caster sugar

1 teaspoon sea salt

1 tablespoon Shaohsing rice wine or dry sherry

1 tablespoon Mijiu rice wine, or vodka or gin

1 spring onion, sliced, to garnish (optional)

FOR THE DRESSING

10 tablespoons Shaohsing rice wine or dry sherry

10 tablespoons juice from the cooked chicken

½ teaspoon toasted sesame oil

1 pinch of sugar

1 pinch of sea salt

1 Wash the chicken and dry with absorbent kitchen paper. Insert the pieces of ginger under the chicken skin.

2 Put the spring onion onto a deep heatproof plate, place the chicken on top and season with the sugar and salt. Pour over both the rice wines or substitutes.

3 Place the plate in a bamboo steamer, cover with a lid and steam over a pan of simmering water (making sure the water does not touch the base of the steamer) on medium heat for about 35 minutes (depending on the size of the chicken thighs). Check the water during cooking – add more if necessary.

4 Test to see if the chicken is cooked, then remove the plate from the steamer. Pour the chicken juices into a bowl and leave to cool. Put the chicken to one side to cool.

5 Place all the ingredients for the dressing in a large bowl and stir to combine.

6 Once the chicken is cool to the touch, you can either remove the skin or leave it on. Chop the meat into bite-sized pieces, add to the dressing and cover the bowl. Place in the fridge for several hours, and preferably overnight, before serving. Garnish with spring onion, if you like, and serve.

Ching's tip

To make this as a salad, cook the chicken in the same way but once cooked, shred it with your fingers. Add to the dressing with some finely sliced cucumber and carrot strips and top with finely chopped spring onions. Chill as above. If I could get my hands on jellyfish, it would be the perfect accompaniment to this particular type of salad – crunchy and delicious.

My crispy duck is inspired by the popular Sichuan favourite. The duck is first seasoned and then pan-fried until the skin is crispy; the cooking is then finished off in the oven. I like serving this with a sweet and sour apricot and plum sauce. This dish is delicious accompanied by stir-fried green beans and roasted sweet potatoes.

Crispy duck

SERVES 2

2 duck breasts, skin on, skin scored in a
   criss-cross pattern
1 tablespoon groundnut oil
soy and sesame French beans (see page
   159) and roast sweet potatoes (see
   page 168) to serve

FOR THE MARINADE

4 tablespoons freshly grated root ginger
2 tablespoons Shaohsing rice wine or
   dry sherry
2 tablespoons ground Sichuan
   peppercorns

2 tablespoons sea salt
6 star anise
1 tablespoon dark soy sauce
1 tablespoon light soy sauce

FOR THE APRICOT AND PLUM SAUCE

100ml/3½fl oz water
2 plums, quartered and stoned
50g/2oz dried apricots, chopped
2 tablespoons sugar
1 tablespoon runny honey
1 cinnamon stick
1 star anise
juice of 1 lime

1 Put all the ingredients for the marinade into a bowl and stir to combine. Add the duck, cover with clingfilm and leave to marinate for 20 minutes.

2 Preheat the oven to 200°C/400°F/gas mark 6. Heat a wok or pan over a high heat and add the groundnut oil. Place the duck into the wok or pan, skin side down, and fry for 4–5 minutes until the skin is brown and crisp. Transfer to a baking tray, skin side up, and cook in the oven for 3–4 minutes (depending on how well done you like the duck).

3 While the duck is in the oven, make the apricot and plum sauce. Put the water into a small pan and bring to the boil. Add the plums, apricots, sugar, honey, cinnamon and star anise and cook until reduced to a sticky sauce. Take off the heat and stir in the lime juice.

4 To serve, place a duck breast on each plate, pour the sauce over and serve with the beans and sweet potatoes.

I have used dofu ru as a rub on lamb chops, like a marinade – it gives the meat a gorgeous rounded beany flavour, which is unique and really tasty. In Hong Kong, the wet market stalls sell all kinds of bean curd and plenty of dofu ru. I was unable to bring a jar back during my travels but I found some in my local Chinese supermarket. These dofu ru lamb chops served with my adzuki red bean and butter bean mash could not be any easier; adzuki beans are high in protein and can now be found ready cooked in tins in supermarkets – hooray!

Lamb chops in dofu ru with adzuki and butter bean mash

SERVES 2

6 cubes of spiced red dofu ru
600g/1lb 5oz lamb loin chops (about 6 chops)
2 garlic cloves, minced
2 tablespoons groundnut oil
50ml/2fl oz light soy sauce blended with
   1 teaspoon soft light brown sugar
sea salt and ground black pepper

FOR THE GARLIC MUSHROOMS

100ml/3½fl oz Cabernet Sauvignon wine
1 garlic clove, finely chopped
1 tablespoon Chinkiang black rice vinegar
   or balsamic vinegar
250g/9oz mixed oyster mushrooms

FOR THE BEAN MASH

2 tablespoons groundnut oil
235g tin adzuki red beans, drained
235g tin butter beans, drained
2 tablespoons Chinkiang black rice
   vinegar or balsamic vinegar
3 tablespoons light soy sauce
1 teaspoon dried chilli flakes
dash of toasted sesame oil
ground white pepper
1 handful of fresh coriander, leaves
   and stalks, finely chopped

1 Rub a cube of dofu ru on each chop and then rub in the garlic. Place the chops on a plate, cover with clingfilm and leave in the fridge to marinate for as long as possible – overnight is ideal, but 20 minutes is okay if you are short of time.

2 When ready to cook, season the chops with salt and pepper. Heat a wok or pan over a high heat and add the groundnut oil. Add the lamb chops and cook until browned on one side, then turn them over and cook to brown the other side.

3 Reduce the heat to medium, pour in the soy sauce and sugar mixture and let the sauce reduce. If you like your lamb quite rare, you can remove it from the pan once the sauce has reduced to a slightly sticky consistency – 1–2 minutes. If you like your lamb well done, transfer the chops to a baking tray and finish off in the oven at 200°C/400°F/gas mark 6 for 6–8 minutes, depending on the size of the chops.

4 For the garlic mushrooms, pour the wine into the wok or pan, add the garlic and vinegar and stir-fry for 1 minute to reduce the sauce. Add the oyster mushrooms and cook for 1 minute until slightly softened. Remove from the heat and put to one side.

5 To make the bean mash, heat a pan and add the groundnut oil, then add the red beans and butter beans and mix well, breaking up the beans lightly with the back of a wooden spoon. Add the vinegar, soy sauce, chilli flakes, sesame oil and pepper and mix well. Lastly, add the chopped coriander and mix well.

6 To serve, spoon a serving of bean mash onto each plate, place three lamb chops on the mash, top with a large spoonful of the garlic mushrooms and drizzle the sauce over the dish.

This recipe was said to be an imperial dish that the emperor ate. Once cooked, the meatballs, surrounded by Chinese cabbage, are said to resemble the head of the lion, while the cabbage resembles the 'mane'. My mother cooked this dish when I was younger and told us that we would be as strong as lions if we ate it.

Lionhead meatballs

MAKES 12

100ml/3½fl oz groundnut oil
750ml/1¼ pints water or vegetable stock
300g/11oz Chinese cabbage/leaf,
   quartered lengthways from leaf to stem
3 dried Chinese mushrooms
1 tablespoon light soy sauce
1 tablespoon cornflour blended with
   2 tablespoons cold water (optional)
2 large spring onions, sliced
sea salt and ground white pepper
steamed jasmine rice (see page 156)
   to serve

FOR THE MEATBALLS

500g/1lb 2oz minced beef
4 garlic cloves, finely chopped
2 tablespoons freshly grated root
   ginger
2 spring onions, finely chopped
½ teaspoon sea salt
50ml/2fl oz Shaohsing rice wine or
   dry sherry
2 tablespoons light soy sauce
1 tablespoon toasted sesame oil
1 egg, beaten
1 tablespoon cornflour
1 pinch of ground white pepper

1 Put all the ingredients for the meatballs into a large bowl and stir to combine, stirring in the same direction. Using wetted hands, take a large mound of the minced meat mixture and mould into a ball a little larger than a golf ball. Place on a plate and repeat with the remaining mixture.

2 Pour the groundnut oil into a large deep pan and heat over a high heat. Using a metal ladle, carefully lower each meatball into the oil and spoon some of the oil over the meatballs. Cook for 4–5 minutes until browned.

3 Pour all but 2 tablespoons of oil out into a heatproof bowl. Add the water or stock to the pan. Arrange the slices of Chinese cabbage around the meatballs, curving them around the sides of the pan lengthways, then add the mushrooms and soy sauce and bring to the boil. Cover the pan, reduce the heat and cook gently for 15 minutes. Add the blended cornflour, if using, and stir until thickened.

4 Take off the heat, season to taste with salt and pepper and sprinkle with the spring onions. Transfer to a serving dish and serve immediately with steamed rice.

In the Sichuan province the rivers are abundant with carp and other freshwater fish, and so, traditionally, fish dishes based on saltwater fish were never cooked, except for those using preserved dried seafood – clams, scallops and mussels. Many varieties of carp can be found in this province and these days a lot of seafood is flown in from the nearby coasts, giving cooks access to fresh saltwater fish. This region also has a love of using chilli bean sauce, made from chillies and broad beans fermented with salt to produce a deep brown red sauce. You have been warned – this recipe is bursting with heat!

Steamed carp coated in spicy bean curd sauce

SERVES 2

2.5cm/1 inch piece of fresh root ginger, peeled and sliced
1 large whole carp, de-scaled, cleaned, skin slashed on both sides
1 tablespoon Shaohsing rice wine or dry sherry
1 large spring onion, sliced at an angle
300g/11oz baby white-stemmed pak choy, sliced into halves along the stem
steamed jasmine rice (see page 156) to serve

FOR THE SPICY BEAN CURD SAUCE

2 tablespoons groundnut oil
2 garlic cloves, crushed and finely chopped
2 tablespoons freshly grated root ginger
1 medium red chilli, deseeded and finely chopped
1 tablespoon chilli bean sauce
200ml/7fl oz hot vegetable stock
200g/7oz fresh firm bean curd (dofu), cut into 1cm/$\frac{1}{2}$ inch cubes
1 tablespoon light soy sauce
1 pinch of sugar
1 tablespoon cornflour blended with 2 tablespoons cold water

FOR THE GARNISH

3 tablespoons dry-roasted peanuts or toasted cashew nuts
1 large spring onion, finely chopped
fresh coriander sprigs

1 Place the ginger in the slashes in the skin on both sides of the fish. Put the carp on a heatproof plate and place inside a bamboo steamer (see Ching's tip). Pour the rice wine or sherry over the fish and spread the sliced spring onion over the top of it. Put the lid on the steamer and place the steamer over a pan of boiling water (making sure the water does not touch the base of the steamer). Steam for 7–8 minutes, depending on the size of the fish, until the skin breaks easily when poked lightly. Turn the heat off and leave the fish in the steamer to keep warm.

2 A few minutes before the fish is cooked, add another layer to the bamboo steamer, put the pak choy on a small heatproof plate and steam together with the fish.

3 To make the sauce, heat a wok over a high heat and add the groundnut oil. Add the garlic, ginger and chopped chilli and stir-fry for less than 1 minute. Stir in the chilli bean sauce followed by the hot vegetable stock, then add the bean curd and season with the soy sauce and sugar. Bring the sauce to the boil, add the blended cornflour and stir to thicken the sauce. Take off the heat.

4 To serve, transfer the fish onto a serving plate and arrange the pak choy halves around it. Pour the spicy bean curd sauce over the fish and garnish with the peanuts, spring onion and coriander sprigs. Serve immediately. Steamed rice would go well with this dish.

Ching's tip

If you don't have a large enough steamer, place the fish on a heatproof plate and put on a roasting rack in a tin. Put the tin in the oven and carefully pour boiling water into the tin. Cover with foil and cook for 7–8 minutes at 200°C/400°F/gas mark 6, or until the flesh flakes when poked and has turned opaque.

Historically, Beijing relied upon the neighbouring provinces of Hebei, Tianjin and Shandong for its seafood and other fresh produce, which because of the transportation involved were preserved using various drying methods. However, today with modern transportation, produce from Shandong can arrive in the markets in Beijing within a day and fresh catches such as sea bass are a prized restaurant dish. A particularly popular dish is steamed fish served in a soy and spring onion hot oil, which originated from southern China where steaming is a common cooking technique. I have made my version of steamed sea bass cooked with a beer sauce. Try it with rice and my stir-fried garlic pak choy (see page 159).

Steamed sea bass in hot beer and ginger lime sauce

SERVES 2 TO SHARE

2.5cm/1 inch piece of fresh root ginger, peeled and cut into long thin strips

1 whole wild sea bass (550g/1¼lb), de-scaled, gutted, cleaned and skin scored, or any firm white-fleshed fish

2 tablespoons Shaohsing rice wine or dry sherry

steamed jasmine rice (see page 156) to serve

FOR THE HOT BEER AND GINGER LIME SAUCE

2 tablespoons groundnut oil

1 tablespoon freshly grated root ginger

zest of 1 lime

330ml bottle Chinese beer (Tsingtao)

2 tablespoons light soy sauce

2 spring onions, sliced into long strips

1 large handful of fresh coriander, leaves and stalks, roughly chopped

For the method, please see overleaf.

1 Either drape some of the ginger strips across the fish or tuck them within the scores in the skin, then put the rest inside the fish. Place the fish on a heatproof plate or dish (see Ching's tips) and pour the rice wine or sherry over it. Place the plate in a large bamboo steamer (see Ching's tips) and cover, then place on top of a wok or pan of boiling water (making sure the water does not touch the base of the steamer). Steam the fish for 8–10 minutes (depending on the size of the fish) until the flesh flakes when poked with chopsticks. Turn off the heat and leave the fish in the steamer.

2 To make the sauce, heat a large pan or wok and heat the groundnut oil. Add the ginger and stir-fry for a few seconds, then add the lime zest, followed by the beer and soy sauce. Stir and, as the liquid comes to the boil, add the spring onions and coriander, then take off the heat immediately.

3 Remove the plate and fish from the bamboo steamer, pour the sauce over the fish and serve immediately with steamed rice.

Ching's tips

When choosing the dish for steaming the sea bass, choose one that you are happy to use as a serving dish, too (this saves having to transfer the fish and means less washing up), but it should be heatproof. Also, make sure that the dish is deep enough to hold all the delicious sauce.

If you don't have a large enough steamer, place the fish on a heatproof plate and put on a roasting rack in a tin. Put the tin in the oven and carefully pour boiling water into the tin. Cover with foil and cook for 8–10 minutes at 200°C/400°F/gas mark 6, or until the flesh flakes when poked and has turned opaque.

On a trip to Beijing, I was fortunate to visit a lamasery called Yonghegong. There sits the largest carved Buddha in the world with hundreds of Buddha deities, and Buddhists and non-Buddhists from all over the world come to this special place to pay their respects. My family are Buddhist and we have a tradition that once a month when the moon is roundest (15th of every lunar calendar month) we give up meat as a symbol of our compassion to animals. This is my favourite vegetarian dish and I call it Buddha's stir-fried vegetables because it contains eight vegetables – the number eight is a symbol of the eight noble paths in Buddhism.

Buddha's stir-fried vegetables

SERVES 2

1 tablespoon groundnut oil
2 dried Chinese mushrooms, pre-soaked in cold water for 20 minutes, drained and sliced
1 small carrot, sliced
1 handful of mangetout
1 small handful of deep-fried dofu (bean curd)
1 small handful of dried wood ear mushrooms, pre-soaked in hot water for 20 minutes and drained

1 small handful of baby corn, sliced
1 small handful of bean sprouts
100ml/3½fl oz hot vegetable stock
2 tablespoons light soy sauce
2 tablespoons vegetarian oyster sauce
1 teaspoon toasted sesame oil
1 large spring onion, sliced
1 teaspoon cornflour blended with 1 tablespoon cold water
1 small handful of raw enoki mushrooms
steamed jasmine rice (see page 156) to serve

1 Heat a wok over a high heat, add the groundnut oil and stir-fry the Chinese mushrooms until the fragrance is released.

2 Add the carrot, mangetout, dofu, wood ear mushrooms and baby corn and stir-fry for 1 minute until the vegetables are tender.

3 Add the bean sprouts and hot vegetable stock and season with the soy sauce, oyster sauce and sesame oil. Stir in the spring onion.

4 Bring to the boil, add the blended cornflour and stir until thickened. Add the enoki mushrooms and toss through. Serve with steamed rice.

This is an easy dish that can be made ahead and then kept warm in the oven. Serve as a starter or main course. It is very nutritious and good for you. If you love seafood, you can add some chopped shrimps or scallops and then top each dish with caviar. The result is a golden dish, which can also be served at a Chinese New Year party.

Steamed egg, shiitake mushrooms and seaweed

SERVES 4

8 eggs, beaten

2 teaspoons freshly grated root ginger

4 shiitake mushrooms, diced

1 small spring onion, finely chopped

4 tablespoons finely chopped fresh coriander

2 teaspoons toasted sesame oil

2 teaspoons light soy sauce

1 pinch each of sea salt and ground black pepper

TO GARNISH

4 teaspoons finely cut nori (dried seaweed) or bought crispy seaweed

8 chives, finely chopped

1 Mix all the ingredients, except the garnish, in a bowl.

2 Divide the mixture between four small ceramic rice bowls with lids (or 1 large/600ml/1 pint shallow heatproof serving bowl not more than 4cm/1½ inches deep and small enough to fit into a bamboo steamer).

3 Place 1.4 litres/2½ pints of water into a large wok or pan and bring to the boil. Place the bowl(s) in a steamer set over the wok or pan (making sure the water does not touch the base of the steamer) and steam for 15–20 minutes.

4 To check the egg is cooked, run a toothpick through the egg mixture – it should come out clean.

5 Remove from the steamer, sprinkle each bowl with nori or crispy seaweed and chopped chives and serve immediately.

This delicious vegetarian dish was apparently a favourite of Empress Dowager Cixi of the last Ching dynasty. A northern-style dish, it is a popular classic. The bean curd is first deep-fried and then coated in ginger and rice wine sauce. The dofu is crunchy on the outside but remains soft and tender on the inside, so much so that, when you use fresh bean curd, it melts in your mouth. Do use firm fresh bean curd for this recipe – there is just no substitute. This dish is great accompanied by steamed jasmine rice to soak up the sauce.

Northern-style bean curd (dofu)

SERVES 4

400g/14oz fresh firm dofu, drained and cut into 2.5cm/1 inch cubes
60g/2½oz potato flour or cornflour
groundnut oil for deep-frying
1 egg, lightly beaten
1 spring onion, finely chopped

FOR THE STIR-FRY

1 tablespoon freshly grated root ginger
150ml/5fl oz vegetable stock
1 tablespoon Shaohsing rice wine or dry sherry
½ teaspoon sea salt
1 pinch of sugar
1 teaspoon toasted sesame oil
1 tablespoon cornflour blended with 2 tablespoons cold water (optional)

1 Coat the dofu cubes in potato flour or cornflour and place on a plate.

2 Heat a wok over a high heat and fill to a quarter of its depth with groundnut oil. Heat the oil to 180°C/350°F, or until a cube of bread dropped in turns golden brown in 15 seconds.

3 Coat each dofu cube in the beaten egg and lower into the wok. Cook all the dofu until golden brown, then remove and place on a plate lined with absorbent kitchen paper. Drain the oil from the wok, leaving about 1 tablespoon.

4 Reheat the oil, add the ginger and stir-fry for a few seconds, then add the stock, rice wine or sherry, the salt and sugar and bring to the boil. Add the dofu back into the wok and then drizzle with the sesame oil. For a smoother, slightly thicker sauce, add the blended cornflour when the sauce has come to the boil and stir until thickened before adding the remaining ingredients. Sprinkle the spring onion over the top and serve immediately.

Desserts and
drinks

I adore fruit jellies. They are not only easy and quick to make, they are also great after a fishy or heavy meal and they cleanse the palate nicely. This one is a mixture of my favourite fruits. If you cannot get fresh lychees just use the tinned variety. You can make this alcoholic or non-alcoholic, it's up to you. Try using a sparkling wine or sparkling soft drink – the bubbles are captured when the jelly sets and they then fizz in your mouth when you are enjoying it. Delicious!

Lychee, lime and mixed fruit jelly

FILLS 4 SMALL WINE GLASSES

6 gelatine leaves
100ml/3½fl oz water
200ml/7fl oz lychee juice
juice of 1 lime
1 tablespoon caster sugar
4 lychees, fresh or tinned
8 whole blackberries
4 whole strawberries
4 tablespoons pomegranate seeds
sparkling wine, champagne or natural sparkling soft drink

1 Chill four small wine glasses in the fridge.

2 Place the leaf gelatine in a little cold water and leave for 5 minutes to soften. Lift out and place in a pan with the measured water. Heat gently until the gelatine dissolves.

3 Put the lychee juice, lime juice and caster sugar into another pan. Heat gently to dissolve the sugar, then let it cool slightly. Pour the fruit juice mixture into the gelatine and mix well.

4 Place 1 lychee, 2 blackberries, 1 strawberry and 1 tablespoon pomegranate seeds into each wine glass. Pour the gelatine mixture into each glass, leaving 2.5cm/1 inch space at the top. Top up the rest of the glass with sparkling wine or sparkling soft drink, and then place the glasses in the fridge for 2 hours to chill before serving.

Mmm... this is delectable. Forget savoury spring rolls, sweet ones are here to rule. This will make you think about spring rolls in a different light. Here, sweetened adzuki red beans are used. Alternatively, buy the unsweetened tinned cooked ones and add some runny honey or brown sugar. In fact, if you do not like adzuki red bean, just use banana and some hazelnut spread (or small cubes of milk or dark chocolate) and make banana and chocolate spring rolls!

I promise a Chinese dessert has never tasted so good and it takes just seconds to make.

Red bean paste and banana spring rolls

SERVES 2

10 small spring roll wrappers
210g tin cooked and
 sweetened adzuki red
 bean paste
1 banana, peeled and thinly
 sliced, then slices halved
2 tablespoons groundnut oil

TO SERVE

walnuts
vanilla ice cream
maple syrup

Ching's tip

Instead of spring roll pastry, you can use two 10 x 10cm/4 x 4 inch squares of filo pastry for each wrapper, if you like. Brush one sheet with oil, cover with the second sheet and brush with oil again. Then fill and roll as in step 1.

1 Place a spring roll wrapper on a flat surface, place 2 teaspoons of the red bean paste in the centre and spread the filling across two-thirds of the wrapper, leaving space at one end to seal the spring roll.

2 Place the banana pieces on top of the red bean paste. Fold in the left and right sides of the wrapper towards the middle and then roll up from the filled end. Put onto a plate seam side down. Make the rest of the spring rolls in the same way.

3 Heat a shallow pan and add the groundnut oil. Add the rolls one at a time and shallow-fry, turning them over as the skin crisps up on one side. Remove from the pan and place five on each serving plate.

4 Add the walnuts to the pan and toast them for 30 seconds, then transfer to a board and, using the back of a knife, crush roughly and sprinkle over the spring rolls. Serve immediately with scoops of vanilla ice cream and a drizzle of maple syrup.

I love durian – it is the king of fruits: smelly, thorny and meaty, it is not one for the faint-hearted. You may need to hold your nose whilst eating this dish but I promise you it is divine. These puffs are a real treat – delicious on their own or served as in this recipe. Enjoy!

Durian honey puffs with vanilla ice cream and maple syrup

MAKES 6 PUFFS

350g/12oz ready-rolled puff pastry
250g/9oz durian meat
1 tablespoon runny honey
1 egg, beaten

FOR THE STICKY WALNUTS

100g/3½oz walnuts
200ml/7fl oz golden syrup
5 tablespoons soft dark brown sugar

TO SERVE

vanilla ice cream
icing sugar to dust
drizzle of maple syrup
mint sprigs to decorate (optional)

1 Preheat the oven to 200°C/400°F/gas mark 6. Line two baking trays with greaseproof paper.

2 Roll out the pastry on a wooden board and, using a round 6cm/2¼ inch cutter, cut out 12 pastry circles.

3 Put the durian meat into a small blender, add the honey and whiz to combine. Turn out into a bowl.

4 Place one piece of pastry in the palm of your hand and take a heaped tablespoon of the durian and honey mixture and place it in the centre of the pastry. Place another piece of pastry on top of the first and lightly seal the edges like a dumpling. Place on one of the baking trays. Repeat with the remaining pastry and filling. Brush the pastry tops with egg wash. Bake in the oven for about 15 minutes or until the pastry turns golden brown.

5 Meanwhile, dry-toast the walnuts in a pan and then pour the golden syrup over them. Pour them onto the second baking tray, sprinkle the brown sugar over the top and place them in the oven for 2 minutes to dissolve the sugar. Remove from the oven and leave to cool for 10 minutes. When cooled, the walnuts will have a sweet, crunchy but sticky texture.

6 To serve, place a durian puff on each serving plate and top with a scoop of vanilla ice cream. Dust the dish with icing sugar, then place two or three candied walnuts on the side of the ice cream. Drizzle with maple syrup and garnish with a mint sprig, if you like.

This dessert was inspired by my visit to the Great Wall in Beijing. The walnuts represent the Great Wall, while the ice cream represents the mountains surrounding the wall. The mint sprigs represent the trees next to the wall, and the frosted cornflakes, scattered all over the dish, symbolise autumnal leaves (or use a dusting of icing sugar to symbolise snow in winter!).

Great Wall of China green tea ice cream with candied walnuts

SERVES 2

6 tablespoons Longjing tea leaves, or other green tea leaves, roughly chopped
900ml/1½ pints double cream
100g/3½oz caster sugar

FOR THE CANDIED STICKY WALNUTS

210g/7½oz walnut halves
450g/1lb golden syrup
2 tablespoons soft light brown sugar

TO DECORATE

mint sprigs
frosted cornflakes, roughly crushed

1 Heat a pan over a medium heat, and add the tea leaves, cream and caster sugar. Stir well to dissolve the sugar, then put to one side and leave to cool. Once cooled, transfer to an ice-cream machine and follow the manufacturer's instructions to make ice cream, then transfer to the freezer.

2 When ready to serve, preheat the oven to 200°C/400°F/gas mark 6. Heat a medium pan and dry-toast the walnuts for 1 minute. Add the golden syrup and warm through, stirring to coat the walnuts in the syrup. Line a roasting tin with greaseproof paper, pour the walnuts and syrup in and then sprinkle over the brown sugar. Place in the oven for 3–4 minutes to dissolve the sugar a little – when the sugar cools it will form a glaze and stick the syrup to the walnuts further. Leave these to cool slightly.

3 Divide a large round plate into three sections – imagine three lines leading from the rim of the plate all meeting in the centre. Starting from the centre of the plate and using chopsticks or wetted fingers, place four or five pieces of walnut along each line, then top with three or four, then two or three, and so forth, so that the 'wall' becomes lower as you reach the edge of the plate. Place a generous scoop of ice cream in each of the three sections between the 'walls' and decorate the peaks of the ice cream with mint sprigs. Sprinkle over some crushed cornflakes and serve immediately. Place some dessertspoons to share at the table between two.

Empress Dowager Cixi, of the late Qing dynasty, was a very superstitious woman. If you visit her favourite Summer Palace in Beijing, you will find peach-decorated vases and paintings everywhere. Peaches and nectarines to the Chinese symbolise longevity and sons, and when coupled with clocks and watches symbolise a peaceful and long life. Inspired by this, I made this refreshing peach pudding. If you are superstitious you could place a small antique pocket watch alongside this dish, and you would wish the person you were serving this dessert to a 'long and peaceful middle life' – 'Chong sheng pin an'.

Empress Dowager Cixi's longevity peach pudding

SERVES 2

FOR THE PEACH PUDDING

2 x 235g drained weight tins peaches in syrup
200ml/7fl oz evaporated milk
100g/3½oz caster sugar
12 gelatine leaves
200ml/7fl oz water
single cream to serve (optional)

FOR THE MIXED BERRY FRUIT COMPOTE

1 small handful each of blackberries, raspberries, strawberries and cranberries
1 tablespoon caster sugar

FOR DECORATING

2 ripe nectarines
2 handfuls of crushed ice

1 Purée the peaches with their syrup in a blender. Transfer to a bowl and stir in the evaporated milk, then add the sugar and mix well.

2 Place the leaf gelatine in a little cold water and leave for 5 minutes to soften. Lift out and place in a pan with the measured water. Heat gently until the gelatine dissolves. Pour the gelatine mixture into the peach purée.

3 Ladle the mixture into four serving bowls, cover with clingfilm and refrigerate for 1 hour.

4 Just before serving, make the warmed compote. Heat a small pan, add all the berries to warm through, then add the sugar and stir gently to dissolve.

5 Halve the nectarines, remove the stones and cut into slices. Place the slices in a circular fan on top of the peach purée in the serving bowls. Place a tablespoon of crushed ice in the middle of each, then top with a tablespoon of the compote. Drizzle with cream, if you like, and serve immediately.

Ginger and almonds are popular ingredients in Chinese cookery, but ginger is not often used in desserts. Almonds (flaked, whole or ground), however, have been used to flavour many dessert dishes, from pastries and buns to almond jellies and wholesome nutty breakfast drinks. Here, ground almonds are used to make delicious crunchy cookies, and stem ginger is used in the ice cream. This makes more biscuits than you need, but it does mean more to eat with afternoon tea!

Almond cookies with ginger and vanilla ice cream

SERVES 2

FOR THE GINGER AND VANILLA ICE CREAM

450ml/15fl oz double cream
125g/4oz caster sugar
1 teaspoon vanilla extract
2 vanilla pods
3 pieces of preserved stem ginger, sliced

FOR THE ALMOND COOKIES

115g/3¾oz unsalted butter
150g/5oz caster sugar
1 egg, beaten
150g/5oz sifted plain flour, plus extra to dust
zest of 1 lime
75g/3oz ground almonds
almond essence (if available)

TO SERVE

4 tablespoons Amaretto almond liqueur
fresh mint sprigs
4 fortune cookies

1 First make the ice cream. Pour the cream into a pan and add the caster sugar and vanilla extract. Slice down the middle of each vanilla pod and scrape the seeds out into the pan. Add the ginger, stir the mixture and heat gently until the sugar has dissolved. Take off the heat and leave to cool. When cool, transfer to an ice-cream machine and follow the manufacturer's instructions. Put the ice cream into a container and freeze until ready to serve.

2 Make the almond cookies. Preheat the oven to 180°C/350°F/gas mark 4. Line a baking tray with baking parchment.

3 Put the butter into a large bowl and beat until soft. Add the caster sugar and cream with the butter. Stir in the beaten egg. Add the sifted flour, lime zest, ground almonds and almond essence, if using, and mix to a dough.

4 Turn the dough out onto a floured surface and knead into a ball. Using a floured rolling pin, roll out the dough to a thickness of about 5mm/¼ inch and, using biscuit cutters of your preference, cut out the dough and place the biscuits on the baking tray. Bake for 15 minutes until golden brown, then remove and cool on a wire rack.

5 To serve, crumble a little biscuit into four martini glasses, top with ice cream and pour 1 tablespoon of Amaretto over each one. Decorate with a sprig of mint and serve with a fortune cookie on top of the ice cream. Store the remaining biscuits in an airtight container.

I had this refreshing dessert in Hong Kong and have resurrected it in my version below. This is easy to prepare – make the ice cream in advance and then all you have to do is concentrate on making the jelly. This is a perfect make-ahead dessert and one that is full of flavour.

Mango madness

SERVES 4

FOR THE MANGO ICE CREAM

**900ml/1½ pints double
cream**
100g/3½oz caster sugar
**435g tin mangoes, fruit and
syrup puréed**

FOR THE MANGO JELLY

**435g tin mangoes, strained
and syrup retained**
12 gelatine leaves
200ml/7fl oz water

TO SERVE

4 handfuls of ice cubes
**1 fresh mango, peeled,
stoned and sliced**
fresh mint sprigs (optional)

Ching's tip
Decorate with a crushed fortune cookie, if you like.

1 To make the ice cream, heat the cream in a large pan until medium hot. Add the sugar and puréed mangoes and stir to dissolve the sugar. Take off the heat and put to one side to cool. Once cooled, slowly pour into an ice-cream machine and follow the manufacturer's instructions.

2 Next, make the jelly. Place the mango pieces in a blender and whiz to a purée. Turn out into a bowl.

3 Place the leaf gelatine in a little cold water and leave for 5 minutes to soften. Lift out and place in a pan with the measured water. Heat gently until the gelatine dissolves. Add 100ml/3½fl oz of the dissolved gelatine to the mango purée and the other 100ml/3½fl oz to the mango syrup. Stir well to mix and then pour each separately into two square dishes not larger than 15 x 15cm/6 x 6 inches. Cover the dishes with clingfilm and then refrigerate for 1 hour to set the jelly. When set, using a knife, cut the jelly into 1cm/½ inch square cubes.

4 Before serving, crush the ice cubes in a food processor to make slushed ice.

5 To serve, scoop two or three spoonfuls of mango ice cream into a serving bowl and place 2 tablespoons of crushed ice on top. Place some clear and some yellow mango jelly cubes on top. Decorate with fresh mango slices and a sprig of mint, if you like, and serve immediately.

This is my ultimate East meets West pudding recipe. In China, rice desserts are extremely popular. This is my take on 'Pa-bao fan' ('Eight treasured rice') – eight is a lucky number and treasured ingredients vary from dried citrus peel and dried longan fruit to Chinese dates. Instead of steaming the rice with the ingredients in the traditional way, I cook the rice first, then combine all the ingredients in a wok, spoon them into ramekins and steam again before serving – perfect for making ahead for a feast. I like to serve them with chocolate-coated raisins drizzled with toffee sauce. Forget sticky toffee pudding!

Fruity sticky rice with toffee sauce

SERVES 6

1 tablespoon unsalted butter, plus extra
  to grease
600g/1lb 5oz cooked glutinous rice (see
  page 156)
125g/4oz dates, de-stoned and finely
  chopped
1 large handful of dried golden raisins
  and cranberries
1 tablespoon orange zest

1 tablespoon caster sugar
1–2 tablespoons ground cinnamon

FOR THE TOFFEE SAUCE

2 tablespoons unsalted butter
6 tablespoons soft dark brown sugar
200ml/7fl oz double cream

FOR DECORATION

freshly grated orange zest
1 large handful of chocolate raisins

1 Heat a wok over a medium heat and add the butter. Add the cooked rice, the dates, dried fruit, orange zest, caster sugar and cinnamon and stir to combine well. Turn the heat off.

2 Butter six ramekins. Spoon the rice mixture into the ramekins and fill to the top of each one. These can now be put aside until you are ready to cook them.

3 Before serving, place the ramekins in a bamboo steamer and place over a pan of boiling water. Steam uncovered for 3 minutes until hot. Take off the heat. (If you do not have a steamer, see page 173.)

4 Make the toffee sauce just before serving. Combine the butter, sugar and cream in a pan and heat gently until the butter has melted and the sugar crystals have dissolved.

5 To serve, turn out the ramekins onto a serving plate and drizzle the hot toffee sauce around the steamed rice pudding as well as over the top. Decorate the top with orange zest, sprinkle chocolate raisins around the dessert and serve immediately.

A burst of flavours and colours, this recipe fuses whole rambutans, raspberries and mandarin segments. Traditionally, we eat mandarins or oranges at Chinese New Year as the orange colour symbolises gold and wealth. The Mandarin Chinese word for mandarins/oranges is 'Ju-tse', and 'Tse' is also the homonym for sons/offspring – this is the perfect cocktail to loosen a few buttons and help with that process then! The raspberry makes the cocktail slightly reddy-pink in colour, which is dubbed the luckiest colour according to the Chinese. Lychees make an exotic alternative to rambutans.

Rambutan, raspberry and mandarin mojito

MAKES 8 X 225ML/8FL OZ, EACH SERVED IN A TALL COCKTAIL GLASS

mint leaves from a large
bunch, plus extra to
decorate
2 limes, each cut into
8 wedges
125g/4oz frozen raspberries
24 rambutans or lychees,
fresh or tinned,
8 tablespoons caster sugar
2 good handfuls of ice cubes,
plus extra to serve
250ml/9fl oz white rum
1.4 litres/2½ pints soda
water
3 large mandarins,
segmented

1 Chill 8 tall cocktail glasses in the fridge.

2 Place the mint leaves into a large measuring jug. Add the lime wedges, raspberries, rambutans or lychees and the sugar and use the end of a rolling pin to squash the ingredients together.

3 Add the ice and pour over the rum. Slowly add the soda water and stir well.

4 Put 2 ice cubes into each glass. Top each glass with the cocktail and decorate with mint leaves and mandarin segments. Place a straw in each glass and serve immediately.

These are sophisticated, lightly spiced, delicate teas that make the perfect accompaniment to sweet desserts, or you can drink them on their own. They're great to serve at the end of a dinner party. You can buy dried rose buds in Traditional Chinese Medicine shops, or order online from tea specialists. Alternatively, use a pinch of ground cinnamon. If you're feeling experimental, use a 1cm/½ inch cube of rock sugar instead of honey in the Cinnamon tea. It's also just as good without the honey. And you can substitute lychees for the rambutans if you prefer.

Cinnamon, rambutan, honey and rose bud tea

MAKES 1 CUP

3 dried rose buds
3 rambutans (fresh or tinned)
2 x 5cm/2 inch long pieces
of cinnamon stick, 1cm/
½ inch wide
1 generous teaspoon runny
honey
200ml/7fl oz hot water

1 Place the rose buds, rambutans, cinnamon and honey in a mug or teacup, pour the hot water over and stir well. To enjoy the tea at its best, leave to infuse for 1 minute, then serve.

Goji berry, dried date and rose bud tea

MAKES 1 CUP

1 tablespoon dried goji berries
3 dried Chinese dates or dried
prunes
3 dried rose buds
2cm/¾ inch cube of rock sugar
or 1 generous teaspoon
runny honey
300ml/10fl oz hot water

1 Place the goji berries, dates, rose buds and rock sugar or honey in a mug or teacup. Pour the hot water over and stir well.

2 To enjoy the tea at its best, leave to infuse for 1 minute, then serve.

Rice

Steamed jasmine rice

SERVES 4

**350g/12oz jasmine rice,
washed until the water
runs clear**

600ml/1 pint water

1 Place the rice in a heavy-based saucepan and add the water. Bring to the boil and then cover with a tight-fitting lid and reduce to a low heat. Cook for 15–20 minutes.

2 Uncover the pan and remove from the heat. Fluff up the rice grains with a fork and serve immediately.

Basic glutinous rice

SERVES 4

**300g/11oz washed glutinous
rice**

500ml/18fl oz water

1 Heat a pan, add the rice and water, cover and cook on high heat for 15 minutes. Turn the heat to very low and cook for a further 3 minutes, making sure all the water has evaporated. Take off the heat and, using a spatula, fluff the rice and it is now ready to serve or use.

Beijing rice

SERVES 4

2 tablespoons groundnut oil

3 eggs, beaten

**400g/14oz cooked jasmine rice
(see above)**

3 ripe salad tomatoes, sliced

3 tablespoons light soy sauce

1 tablespoon toasted sesame oil

1 pinch of ground white pepper

**1 large spring onion, finely
sliced**

1 Heat a non-stick wok (to prevent the eggs from sticking) over a high heat and add the groundnut oil. Add the eggs and scramble for a few minutes, then add the rice and stir well to break it up. Add the tomatoes and stir-fry for a few minutes.

2 Season with the soy sauce, sesame oil and pepper. Add the spring onion, mix well and serve immediately.

Stir-fried garlic pak choy

SERVES 4 TO SHARE

1 tablespoon groundnut oil
4 garlic cloves, finely
   chopped
350g/12oz baby pak choy,
   washed and sliced in half
1 generous pinch of salt

1 Heat a wok over a high heat and add the groundnut oil. Add the garlic and pak choy and stir-fry for 2–3 minutes until softened and wilted. Season with salt and serve immediately.

Soy and sesame French beans

SERVES 4 TO SHARE

1 tablespoon groundnut oil
1 garlic clove, finely chopped
400g/14oz French beans,
   washed and trimmed
1 tablespoon light soy sauce
1 tablespoon toasted sesame
   oil
1 small handful of black and
   white sesame seeds or
   mixed health seeds
1 tablespoon pickled red
   cabbage (optional)

1 Heat a wok over a high heat and add the groundnut oil. Add the garlic and stir-fry for a few seconds, then add the French beans and stir-fry for 2–3 minutes. Season with soy sauce and sesame oil.

2 Place on a plate, sprinkle over the sesame seeds and the pickled red cabbage, if you like, and serve immediately.

Choi sum with dried shrimps

SERVES 2

1 tablespoon groundnut oil

2 garlic cloves, crushed and finely chopped

3 dried Chinese mushrooms, pre-soaked in hot water for 20 minutes, drained and sliced

1 small handful of dried shrimps, pre-soaked in hot water for 20 minutes and drained (or use fresh)

300g/11oz choi sum, washed and sliced into 5cm/2 inch lengths

½ teaspoon chilli sauce

1 tablespoon light soy sauce

1 teaspoon toasted sesame oil

1 Heat a wok over a high heat and add the groundnut oil. Add the garlic and stir-fry for a few seconds, then add the mushrooms and stir-fry for a minute until fragrant. Add the shrimps and stir-fry for another minute to release the aroma.

2 Add the choi sum and stir-fry for 1 minute, then season with the chilli sauce, soy sauce and sesame oil and serve immediately.

Choi sum and mixed vegetable salad with pineapple dressing

SERVES 4

200g/7oz choi sum, washed, trimmed and sliced
100g/3½oz sugarsnap peas
2 large carrots, cut into julienne strips
1 red pepper, deseeded and sliced
1 yellow pepper, deseeded and sliced
240g tin of pineapple in natural juice, drained (juice reserved) and sliced
2 spring onions, finely sliced

FOR THE DRESSING

2–3 tablespoons groundnut oil or olive oil
7 tablespoons pineapple juice
2 tablespoons light soy sauce
1 tablespoon clear rice vinegar or cider vinegar
1 pinch of sugar
1 pinch of ground black pepper

1 Prepare all the salad ingredients and toss together in a large serving bowl.

2 Mix all the dressing ingredients in a small bowl and stir well. Pour over the salad, toss well and serve immediately.

Smacked soy and cucumber sesame salad

**1 cucumber, halved
lengthways and deseeded**

**2 garlic cloves, smacked on a
board, and roughly chopped**

**1 carrot, peeled and thinly
sliced at an angle**

**1 tablespoon Chinkiang black
rice vinegar or balsamic
vinegar**

1 tablespoon light soy sauce

**1 tablespoon toasted sesame
oil**

1 pinch of salt

1 pinch of sugar

1 Cut each cucumber half in half again, then, using a cleaver, smack on a chopping board and cut into several pieces.

2 Toss all the ingredients together and chill until ready to serve.

Steamed pak choy with oyster sauce and fried shallots

SERVES 4 TO SHARE

200g/7oz pak choy, washed and trimmed

3 tablespoons oyster sauce

1 tablespoon deep-fried garlic and shallot seasoning (see below, or available from Chinese supermarkets, optional)

1 Place the pak choy on a heatproof plate and put into a bamboo steamer. Place the steamer over a pan of boiling water (making sure the water does not touch the base of the steamer) and steam on a high heat for 2–3 minutes.

2 Drizzle the oyster sauce over the pak choy and let the latent heat from the vegetables warm the sauce. Sprinkle the deep-fried garlic and shallot seasoning over the top, if you like, and serve immediately.

Ching's tip
You can use gailan (Chinese kale/broccoli) instead of the pak choy, if you prefer.

Deep-fried garlic and shallot seasoning

MAKES ABOUT 135G/4½OZ

400ml/14fl oz groundnut oil or vegetable oil

6 garlic cloves, chopped or sliced

1 small onion, diced

4 small shallots, diced

potato flour or cornflour

1 Heat a wok over a high heat and add the groundnut oil. Heat the oil to 180°C/350°F, or until a cube of bread dropped in turns golden brown in 15 seconds.

2 Dust the garlic, onion and shallots in the flour or cornflour and shake in a sieve to get rid of any excess flour. Using a slotted spider, lower the pieces into the wok and deep-fry for about 15 minutes until golden brown, then lift out and drain on absorbent kitchen paper. Once cooled, transfer to an airtight container until ready to use. Use within 2–3 weeks.

Black bean mushrooms

SERVES 4 TO SHARE

1 tablespoon groundnut oil

2 garlic cloves

1 tablespoon finely chopped fresh root ginger

1 medium red chilli, deseeded and finely chopped

1 tablespoon fermented black beans, washed and crushed

400g/14oz mixed oriental mushrooms, sliced

200ml/7fl oz hot vegetable stock

1–2 tablespoons light soy sauce

1 tablespoon cornflour blended with 2 tablespoons cold water

1 spring onion, finely chopped

1 Heat a wok over a high heat and add the groundnut oil. Add the garlic, ginger and chilli and stir-fry for a few seconds, then add the black beans, followed by the mushrooms and stir-fry for 1–2 minutes.

2 Add the stock and season with soy sauce. Add the blended cornflour and stir well to thicken the sauce. Sprinkle on the spring onion and serve immediately.

Black vinegar oyster mushrooms

SERVES 2

1 tablespoon groundnut oil
200g/7oz oyster mushrooms, sliced
1 tablespoon Chinkiang black rice vinegar or balsamic vinegar
½ teaspoon light soy sauce

1 Heat a wok over a high heat and add the groundnut oil. Add the mushrooms and stir-fry for 1 minute. Season with the vinegar and soy sauce and serve immediately.

Soy and pepper Chinese and chestnut mushrooms

SERVES 2 TO SHARE

1 tablespoon groundnut oil
1 garlic clove, finely chopped
300g/11oz dried Chinese mushrooms, pre-soaked in hot water for 20 minutes, drained, washed and sliced, or sliced chestnut mushrooms
1 tablespoon light soy sauce
1 tablespoon toasted sesame oil
1 pinch each of salt and cracked black pepper

1 Heat a wok over a high heat and add the groundnut oil. Add the garlic and stir-fry for a few seconds. Add the mushrooms and stir-fry for 2 minutes.

2 Season with the soy sauce, sesame oil, salt and pepper to taste. Serve immediately.

Smoked paprika roast sweet potatoes

SERVES 2

2 tablespoons olive oil
½ teaspoon sea salt
1 teaspoon smoked paprika
ground black pepper
350g/12oz sweet potatoes,
peeled and cut into chunks

1 Preheat the oven to 180°C/350°F/gas mark 4.

2 Place the olive oil, salt, smoked paprika and pepper into a roasting tin. Add the sweet potatoes and turn to coat in the seasoned oil, then roast in the oven for 30 minutes and serve immediately.

Red pepper and sweet chilli sauce

SERVES 2

**1 red pepper, deseeded and
    sliced into strips**
olive oil
**5 tablespoons sweet chilli
    sauce**
1 teaspoon lime juice
**sea salt and ground black
    pepper**

1 Preheat the oven to 200°C/400°F/gas mark 6.

2 Place the sliced pepper on a baking tray, drizzle with
   some olive oil and season with salt and pepper.
   Roast for 10 minutes. Remove from the oven.

3 Put the roasted red pepper, sweet chilli sauce and lime
   juice in a bowl and blend well. Chill until ready to use.

Wasabi mayo

SERVES 2

**1 teaspoon wasabi powder
    (see Ching's tip)**
1 tablespoon water
3 tablespoons mayonnaise
1 pinch of caster sugar

1 Mix the wasabi powder with the water and
   mayonnaise in a small bowl, season with the sugar
   and it's ready to use.

Ching's tip
You can use creamed horseradish if you can't find
wasabi powder. Just mix 1 teaspoon with the
mayonnaise and sugar, omitting the water.

Cooking techniques and storecupboard

Essential information you should know before cooking

THE TRUSTED RELIABLE WOK

It has been around for centuries and there is nothing more traditional in Chinese cooking than using the wok. This great invention has been used to help feed millions of people all over the world.

Woks come in various sizes and are made from different materials, and so it can be challenging knowing which to choose. Traditional cast-iron woks are quite heavy and they require seasoning, which is not too difficult. The wok comes coated with a film of oil; wash this off using a sponge and washing up liquid, then dry the wok by placing it over a high flame on the stove. Next, add a little oil (sesame oil is good because it burns quickly) and then use absorbent kitchen paper (hold with a pair of tongs if you wish) to rub in the oil over the entire wok, giving it a darkened blackened effect. Once your wok is seasoned, don't use a metal scourer or iron wool on it, as you will take off the seasoning. If you have never tried this, and you are a keen cook, I would recommend it – there is real pleasure in releasing the 'Wok-hei' or 'smoky' flavour when using a traditional wok.

For those who prefer a lighter wok, I would highly recommend one made from carbon steel (especially for ladies) and you would season it in the same way as a traditional cast-iron wok. If you are short of time, like me, buy a non-stick wok made from carbon steel, which is just as good. A non-stick wok will require less oil for cooking than a cast-iron wok, so is healthier, too.

I prefer a one-handled wok with a medium handle that is not too thick to hold. When choosing your wok, make sure it feels comfortable and right for you. In terms of size, go for a medium one, between 30.5cm/12 inches and 40.5cm/16 inches in diameter that will hold a medium-sized bamboo steamer quite comfortably and allow you to cook up a decent portion to serve at least four.

For those who don't have a gas stove, I would say invest in a new cooker! I find that electric stoves are just not right for wok cooking – sure, you can buy the flat-bottomed wok, but you never really get enough heat to cook the food. You could invest in a good electric wok, which I have used before and found not too bad; these are also good for making hotpots – Chinese-style fondue (see my recipe on page 40).

ONE WOK – SEVERAL TECHNIQUES

STIR-FRYING

This is the ultimate classic experience with using a wok. The amazing thing is that a touch of oil and lots of stirring ensure that the ingredients keep their crunch and take on a smoky flavour. Delish. There are some things to observe, though, to help you cook your dish to perfection.

1 Preparation

Make sure that all the ingredients are prepared in advance, because once you start cooking, you won't have time to stop, otherwise you will burn the food!

A good trick is to cut all the meat to the same size – this ensures that the pieces cook in the same time and retain some of their juices. This same principle also applies to vegetables. For leafy vegetables, cut them on the diagonal – this exposes them to more heat in the wok and they will cook more rapidly.

2 Choosing the right oil

Most oils with a high heating point are great, such as sunflower oil, groundnut oil and vegetable oil, but try to avoid sesame oil as this has a low heating point and burns quickly – save this for seasoning your dishes. Olive oil isn't ideal as it imparts an olive flavour that does not suit all Chinese dishes (although I have used it in one or two recipes). It is best to use a flavourless oil. My favourite is groundnut oil as it has a slight nutty aroma that is not strong enough to overpower a dish, but acts as a great base on which to create the layers of flavours.

3 The correct heat

Prepare the wok for stir-frying by heating it to a high heat and then add the oil and swirl it around in the wok. When the wok starts to smoke you know it's ready to use.

During the cooking process, keep an eye on the flame and level of heat in the wok – you want it high enough so that it sears the food but you do not want to burn the ingredients. You may need to adjust the flame because the temperature will fall in the wok once the ingredients have been added.

4 Order of ingredients and timing

Add the Chinese essentials such as garlic, ginger and chillies first. Secondly, add the meat or seafood, and then, lastly, the vegetables, with a few sprinkles of water to help create steam. This order of cooking helps to retain the bite of the vegetables. An important note to remember is to dry the ingredients before you add them to the wok or the oil will spit, and if there is too much moisture, the ingredients stew rather than 'fry'. When you make a saucy stir-fry and use meats marinated in sauces, just hold back the marinade until the very end of the stir-frying process to make sure it doesn't all evaporate, and again you don't want to stew the food.

A popular technique in the kitchens of Chinese restaurants is to first cook the meat/protein and then scoop it out while the vegetables are stir-fried. The meat/protein is then returned to the wok for the final mixing with seasoning. In the home, I find that you don't always have to cook in this way (as recipes vary), and there are certain dishes where you can add the meat/protein after the garlic, ginger and chillies and then, once they start to cook, you can add the rest of the ingredients; this helps to ensure the meat/protein is not overly cooked. So timing is important in wok cooking – knowing when the ingredient is ready for seasoning and when to add other ingredients. Work with what is best for you, practice makes perfect!

5 Adding cooked ingredients

Cooked noodles/cooked rice can be added at the end and combined with the rest of the ingredients together with all the seasoning.

STEAMING

1 Make sure the wok is stable

For those cooking on a gas stove, invest in a wok rest; this helps to keep the wok stable and secure, especially when steaming and deep-frying.

2 Filling the wok with water

Fill the wok half full with water and place the bamboo steamer over the top, making sure the water in the wok does not touch the base of the steamer. Place the food to be steamed directly inside the steamer (depending on the recipe) or on a heatproof plate that fits in the steamer. Put the lid on and steam. If the recipe requires steaming for a lengthy period of time, top up the wok with more boiling water as necessary. The food cooked in a bamboo steamer is delightful as it takes on a subtle bamboo fragrance. This is another wonderfully healthy way of preparing a meal; it's fast and fun, too. You can also serve your food in the steamer, with the lid on; this helps to keep the food warm for longer.

3 Size of the bamboo steamer

Bamboo steamers vary in size, so make sure that you buy one that sits snugly across the wok and will not touch the water when this is added. If necessary, you can sit the steamer on a heatproof plate, bowl, or rack in the wok to raise it above the water. For those who love to cook a feast, you can pile the steamers on as high as you want (although you need a powerful flame that can induce enough steam to reach the highest steamer; I would say two or three piled high should be okay).

4 A final tip

Make sure that you always turn the flame off under the wok before you attempt to take the lid off the steamer. I have been impatient many times and have burnt my hands and arms from the hot steam.

Note: If you don't have a large enough bamboo steamer for the ingredient you want to cook (such as a large fish), place the food on a heatproof plate and put on a rack in a roasting tin. Carefully pour boiling water into the tin, then cover with foil and place in the oven. Cook for the time stated in the recipe at 200°C/400°F/gas mark 6.

DEEP-FRYING

1 Make sure the oil is hot enough

This may not be a very healthy way of cooking but my tip is that if the oil is hot enough, once the food is dropped in, it cooks at such a high temperature that the outside edges are almost 'sealed', not allowing the ingredient to absorb any more oil, and the high heat continues to cook the inside of the food. To get the best results from deep-frying, make sure you use a deep-frying thermometer. If the oil is too cold, the food will take longer to cook and the result is oily food. If the temperature is too hot, the food will burn and will be undercooked on the inside. If you don't have a thermometer, then you can use the 'bread test', which I refer to in my recipes. Be particularly careful when deep-frying in a wok – don't overfill it, or leave it unattended.

2 Use a spider/mesh and drain well any excess oil on absorbent kitchen paper

A useful trick is to use a fab utensil called a 'spider'. It is a web-like, woven steel mesh scooper that works well as a strainer. It is a godsend for lifting fried foods from the wok (draining much oil in the process) onto dishes lined with kitchen paper (again, to help drain excess oil). The 'spider' comes in different sizes and you should be able to find them in all good Chinese supermarkets and kitchen/cookware shops. They often have a handle made of bamboo.

3 Golden rules

- Make sure the wok is stable, or use a wok stand.
- Make sure there isn't too much oil (less than half full in a wok is maximum) and then there is less chance of bubbling and spilling over.
- Make sure the food is dry, as this prevents spitting.
- For best results, never re-use oil.
- Get your hands on a large, long pair of bamboo chopsticks to help you turn food over if necessary (not plastic chopsticks, as they melt).
- Finally, once you have cooked the dish, serve fried food immediately as it will start to lose its crunch and crispness. However, if necessary, keep the food hot in a preheated oven before serving.

OTHER COOKING UTENSILS

The following would also be useful to have in the kitchen:

Wok cover

Invest in a wok cover; this will allow you to stew, steam, boil and smoke food using your wok. It should have a small top handle to allow you to lift it off, and it should fit snug and firm on the wok.

Wok brush

This is a wooden brush with long hard bristles that is used with hot water to clean the wok. If you cannot get hold of one, don't worry – use a sponge instead.

Chinese spatula /wooden spoon

Traditionally, the metal spatula is used in the Chinese kitchen to allow you to manoeuvre the food and scoop it out of the wok. This is okay for seasoned woks, but you may end up scratching off the non-stick coating if you use a non-stick coated wok. I would suggest a wooden spoon as an alternative.

Ladle

The Chinese ladle is small and bowl-shaped to allow you to collect soups and sauces from the wok, but I would recommend just a normal ladle and not necessarily made from carbon steel as they can rust easily. I would go for one that is made from stainless steel.

Chinese cleaver/good knife

It is essential to invest in a good knife. I usually use a medium chef's knife that is made from stainless steel and is one continuous piece of metal. However, I also have a stainless steel Chinese cleaver with a wooden handle. Cleavers are particularly useful for hacking meat with bones, such as ribs, chopping up chicken, or chopping through roast duck. They are also useful for slicing, shredding, dicing, mincing and mashing (by using the side of the blade and mashing the ingredient between the blade and the chopping board). Of course, you can use a food processor but I find it is good therapy to use the cleaver – it helps to relieve tension after a busy day!

Cutting board

Choose a solid, large wooden chopping board and make sure you clean it well after use. I usually keep three different boards: one for meat, one for seafood, and one for fruit and vegetables.

THE STORECUPBOARD

My top ten essential Chinese storecupboard ingredients:

1. Light soy sauce
2. Dark soy sauce
3. Shaohsing rice wine
4. Toasted sesame oil
5. Five-spice powder
6. Sichuan peppercorns
7. Chinkiang black rice vinegar
8. Clear rice vinegar
9. Chilli bean sauce
10. Chilli sauce

My favourite ingredients for making sauces:

Chilli oil
Fermented salted black beans
Oyster sauce
Hoisin sauce
Yellow bean sauce

Important flavourings:

Garlic
Fresh root ginger
Coriander
Spring onion
Chillies

Cook with:

Groundnut oil/vegetable oil

Other specialist ingredients:

Dried Chinese mushrooms
Dried baby shrimps
Dried tangerine peel
Dried chilli flakes
Dried Sichuan chillies
Cinnamon stick/bark
Fennel
Cloves
Star anise
Jasmine rice

Ching's menu planner

Chinese New Year Party:

Cocktail

Rambutan, raspberry and mandarin mojito
(page 151)

Starter

Spiced skewered lamb (page 107)
Chicken and vegetable spring rolls (page 70)
'Wonton' noodle soup (page 59)
Roast pork pastry puffs (page 63)
Steamed egg, shiitake mushroom and seaweed
(page 132)

Main

Steamed sea bass in hot beer and ginger lime
sauce (page 129)
Chilli crabs with ginger 'juice' (page 93)
Beijing rice (page 156)
Coriander prawns and Longjing tea (page 90)
Crispy duck (page 120)
Lionhead meatballs (page 125)
Northern-style bean curd (page 135)
Buddha's stir-fried vegetables (page 131)

Dessert

Mango madness (page 149)
Durian honey puffs with vanilla ice cream and
maple syrup (page 141)
Red bean paste and banana spring rolls (page 139)
Fruity sticky rice with toffee sauce (page 150)
Cinnamon, rambutan, honey and rose bud tea
(page 153)

For a quick main meal after work, choose one of the following:

Sichuan orange beef (page 42)
Spicy dofu and edamame beans (page 50)
'Gong bao' or 'Kung po prawns' (page 45)
Mango chicken (page 104)
Chicken and cashew nut stir-fry (page 17)
Chicken chow mein (page 26)
Dan Dan noodles (page 37)
Sour ginger pork and celery rice noodle soup
(page 55)
Sweet and tangy chilli beef (page 29)
Chilli chicken with noodles (page 21)

Romantic dinner for two:

Starter

Five-spice beef and sesame dressing
(page 110)

Main

Lamb chops in dofu ru with adzuki and butter
bean mash (page 122)

Dessert

Red bean paste and banana spring rolls
(page 139)

Friends:

Cocktail

Rambutan, raspberry and mandarin mojito (page 151)

Starter

Chicken and vegetable spring rolls (page 70)

Main

Spicy hotpot (page 40)

Dessert

Empress Dowager Cixi's longevity peach pudding (page 144)

Cocktail party:

Rambutan, raspberry and mandarin mojito (page 151)

Chicken and vegetable spring rolls (page 70)

Roast pork pastry puffs (page 63)

Crispy duck (page 120)

Dan Dan noodles (page 37)

Sichuan crispy chilli pork on lettuce (page 34)

Coriander prawns and Longjing tea (page 90)

Pork and prawn dumplings (page 67)

Marbled tea eggs with oyster sauce (page 101)

Radish and sesame soy noodle salad (page 73)

Black bean steamed scallops with noodles (page 79)

Mum's lobster and mayo brioche (page 86)

Mu shu chicken (page 116)

Smacked soy and sesame cucumber salad (page 163)

Lychee, lime and mixed fruit jelly (page 138)

Red bean paste and banana spring rolls (page 139)

Almond cookies with ginger and vanilla ice cream (page 146)

Children:

Starter

Roast pork pastry puffs (page 63)

Sweet and sour soy pork buns (page 16)

Main

Lionhead meatballs (page 125)

Beijing rice (page 156)

Dessert

Almond cookies with ginger and vanilla ice cream (page 146)

Vegetarian dinner:

Starter

Steamed egg, shiitake mushroom and seaweed (page 132)

Main

Beijing rice (page 156)

Buddha's stir-fried vegetables (page 131)

Spicy dofu and edamame beans (page 50)

Radish and sesame soy noodle salad (page 73)

Northern-style bean curd (page 135)

Dessert

Lychee, lime and mixed fruit jelly (page 138)

For something comforting choose one of the following:

Lionhead meatballs with Beijing rice (page 125)

Seafood congee (page 85)

Grandmother's chicken fried rice (page 18)

Dim sum party:

Roast pork pastry puffs (page 63)

Pork and prawn dumplings (page 67)

Marbled tea eggs with oyster sauce
(page 101)

Chicken and vegetable spring rolls
(page 70)

'Wonton' noodle soup (page 59)

Stir-fried garlic pak choy (page 159)

Pork and mushroom 'water-dumplings'
(page 69)

Durian honey puffs with vanilla ice cream and
maple syrup (page 141)

Lychee, lime and mixed fruit jelly
(page 138)

Red bean paste and banana spring rolls
(page 139)

Sunday lunch:

Starter

Five-spice beef and sesame dressing
(page 110)

Main

Five-spice roast chicken drumsticks
(page 105)

Egg and shiitake mushroom fried rice with
tabasco (page 20)

Soy and sesame French beans (page 159)

Dessert

Mango madness (page 149)

Easy entertaining – meat

Starter

Spiced beef stir-fry topped with spring onion
and coriander (page 113)

Main

Crispy duck (page 120)

Smoked paprika roast sweet potatoes
(page 168)

Soy and sesame French beans (page 159)

Dessert

Great Wall of China green tea ice cream with
candied walnuts (page 143)

Easy entertaining – seafood

Starter

Cleansing clam and daikon soup broth (page 76)

Main

Steamed sea bass in hot beer and lime ginger
sauce (page 129)

Dessert

Lychee, lime and mixed fruit jelly (page 138)

For a healthy meal:

Starter

Spiced skewered lamb (page 107)

Main

Sweet and sour pork (page 24)

Dessert

Empress Dowager Cixi's Longevity Peach pudding
(page 144)

Cinnamon, rambutan, honey and rose bud tea
(page 153)

Glossary

Unless otherwise stated, the ingredient should be available in most high street supermarkets.

Adzuki red bean/red bean paste (tinned)

These are whole red beans the size of small oblong-shaped pearls. They are high in protein. Cooked adzuki red beans, in tins, are available from most supermarkets. Sweet ready-prepared red bean paste, available from Chinese supermarkets, is a popular Chinese dessert filling.

Bamboo shoots (tinned)

Drain tinned bamboo shoots and use them in stir-fries and soups. They are rarely available fresh.

Black rice vinegar – see Chinkiang black rice vinegar

Chilli bean sauce (sauce)

This sauce, mainly used in Sichuan cooking, is made from broad beans and chillies that have been fermented with salt to give a deep brown-red sauce. Some versions include fermented soya beans or garlic. This makes a great stewing sauce but use with caution, as some varieties are extremely hot.

Chilli oil (oil)

This is made from dried red chillies heated in oil to give a spicy orange-red fiery oil. Some chilli oils also contain specks of dried chillies. Available from any Chinese supermarket or you can make your own: heat a wok over a medium heat and add some groundnut oil. Add dried chilli flakes with seeds and heat for 2 minutes. Take off the heat and leave the chilli flakes to infuse in the oil until the oil has completely cooled. Decant into a glass jar with a tight lid and store for a month before using. For a clear oil, pass through a sieve.

Chilli sauce (ingredient/dipping sauce)

This can be used in cooking or as a dipping sauce. There are several varieties; some are flavoured with garlic and vinegar.

Chinese beer

Use a light, clear beer, not too strong. Great for drinking and cooking. Alternatively, use a mild lager.

Chinese broccoli – see Chinese kale

Chinese cabbage (fresh)

Also known as Napa cabbage, Tianjin cabbage or Chinese leaf, it has a delicate sweet aroma with a mild cabbage flavour that disappears when the vegetable is cooked. The white stalk has a crunchy texture and remains succulent even after prolonged cooking. The Koreans mainly use it in their pickled cabbage dish called kimchee.

Chinese chives – see Garlic chives

Chinese five-spice powder (spice)

This is a blend of cinnamon, cloves, Sichuan peppercorns, fennel and star anise. These five spices give the sour, bitter, pungent, sweet and salty flavours in Chinese cooking. This spice works extremely well with meats and in marinades.

Chinese kale, fresh

Chinese kale, also known as gailan or Chinese broccoli, comes in several varieties, some with yellow flowers. In general, they all have large, glossy blue-green leaves with long, thick and crisp chunky stems, different to the common Western flowering dark green broccoli. Gailan is served in most Chinese restaurants simply steamed and drizzled with oyster sauce. A good Western substitute is tender leaf broccoli. Gailan can be bought only at Chinese supermarkets.

Chinese wood ear mushrooms (dried)

These dark brown-black fungi have ear-shaped caps and are very crunchy in texture. They do not impart flavour but add colour and crispness to any dish. They should be soaked in hot water for 20 minutes before cooking – they will double in size. After soaking they should be rinsed well to remove any dirt. Store the dried pieces in a glass jar and seal tightly. Available from Chinese supermarkets.

Chinkiang black rice vinegar (condiment)

Made from fermented rice, this strong aromatic vinegar comes from Jiangsu province, where it is produced in the capital, Nanjing. The taste is mellow and earthy and, when cooked, it gives dishes a wonderful smoky flavour.

Throughout China, vinegar is widely used and there are many varieties. Balsamic vinegar makes a good substitute. Available from Chinese supermarkets.

Cinnamon stick/bark (spice)

This is the dried bark of various trees in the *cinnamomun* family, one of the more common being the Cassia tree. It can be used in pieces or ground. Ground cinnamon adds a sweet woody fragrance to any dish. Cinnamon is also said to have health-giving properties, such as preventing the common cold and aiding digestion.

Cloves (spice)

The clove tree is an evergreen and its dried flower buds are the aromatic spice that is one of the components of Chinese five-spice powder. Cloves are strong and quite pungent. They are also used in Traditional Chinese Medicine to help digestion and promote the healthy function of the stomach, spleen and kidneys.

Congee (dish)

A type of plain soupy rice or rice porridge. Can be combined with scrambled eggs, pickled turnip, salted peanuts, fermented bean curd (dofu ru), pickled cucumbers and chilli-pickled bamboo shoots.

Coriander (fresh)

This is mainly used as a garnish or in soups, stir-fries, stews and cold tossed salads. Both the leaves and stems are used.

Coriander seeds (spice)

The dried seeds of the coriander herb. When ground, they give a distinctive warm citrusy aroma to sweet and savoury dishes.

Cumin (spice)

This is the dried seed of the herb *Cuminum cyminum*, and belongs to the parsley family. When ground it has a distinctive, slightly bitter but warm flavour.

Curry powder (spice)

There are many different blends of curry powder. As well as Chinese five-spice powder, some also include coriander, turmeric, cumin, ginger and garlic.

Daikon or white radish (fresh)

This grows in the ground like a root vegetable, and resembles a large white carrot. It has a peppery and crunchy taste and can be eaten raw, pickled or cooked. Daikon contains vitamin C and diastase, an enzyme that helps digestion. It can be sliced or shredded and added to soups, salads and stir-fries. The Koreans use this vegetable to make kimchee, their famous pickle. Store in a sealed bag – daikon has a pungent smell.

Dark soy sauce (condiment)

Made from wheat and fermented soya beans, dark soy sauce has been aged a lot longer than the light soy variety. It is mellower and less salty in taste than light soy, and is used to give flavour and colour.

Deep-fried dofu (bean curd) (fresh)

This is fresh bean curd that has been deep-fried to a golden brown to make it crispy and crunchy on the outside. Usually found in the chilled sections of Chinese supermarkets.

Dofu – see Fresh bean curd

Dofu ru – see Fermented bean curd

Dried chilli flakes (spice)

These are made from dried whole red chillies, including the seeds, which are crushed into flakes – they give a fiery heat when added to dishes.

Dried Chinese mushrooms (dried)

These have a strong aroma and need to be pre-soaked in hot water for 20 minutes before cooking. They have a slightly salty taste and complement savoury dishes well. After soaking, the stem can be left on or discarded. Available from Chinese supermarkets. Use dried shiitake or porcini mushrooms as a substitute.

Dried seaweed/Nori (dried)

This is sold in thin sheets. It is usually roasted over a flame until it turns black or purple to green before it is packaged. Nori can be used as a garnish or to wrap sushi. Once opened, the pack must be sealed and stored in an airtight container, or the nori can lose its crispness. If this happens, just roast the sheets over an open flame for a few seconds until crisp.

Dried shrimp (dried)

These are shrimp that have been pre-cooked and then dried and salted to preserve them. To use, soak in hot water for 20 minutes to soften them, then drain. Orange-red in colour and very pungent in aroma and taste, they come in packets. As with all preserved ingredients, it is best to store them in an airtight container. Available from Chinese supermarkets.

Dried tangerine peel (spice)

This is used as a flavouring ingredient in braised dishes or master sauces. It does not need to be pre-soaked before cooking, but can be added straight to the cooking liquid. It is sold in bags in Chinese supermarkets. Use fresh orange zest as a substitute.

Durian (fruit)

Durian is native all over southeast Asia and is widely popular. It also has heat-giving 'yang' properties and, to counteract this, mangosteens are usually eaten afterwards (known as the queen of fruits, they have 'yin' cooling properties). The durian has a tough thorny exterior and the only way to get at the flesh is by pressing down the sides where the exterior starts to break apart – a small crack that lets you know the fruit is ripe and ready to eat. Inside the durian there are several compartments containing pale yellow, creamy, custardy, lychee-mango-tasting meat. There are seeds within the meat and these can be removed easily. Available from Chinese supermarkets.

Edamame beans (fresh/frozen)

Edamame are green soy beans that are harvested while the beans are still attached to the bushy branches on which they grow. 'Eda' means 'branches' and 'mame' means 'beans' in Japanese. The pods are cooked whole and the seeds are then squeezed out. Available fresh or frozen.

Egg noodles (fresh/dried)

The most common type of noodle, they are made from egg yolk, wheat flour and salt and come in various thicknesses and shapes. Some are flat and thin, others are long and rounded like spaghetti; some are flat and coiled in a ball. Available in various dried and fresh varieties. Store the fresh variety in the fridge for up to 5 days.

Enoki mushrooms (fresh)

These are tiny, white, very thin, long-stemmed mushrooms with a mild delicate flavour. When raw, they give great texture to salads. When lightly steamed, they are slightly chewy. They require very little cooking.

Fennel seeds (spice)

Fennel is a strong aromatic spice that has a slight aniseed aroma and flavour, but is much sweeter. It is one of the ingredients in Chinese five-spice powder. Delicious when toasted or pan-fried and added to dishes.

Fermented bean curd (dofu ru) (preserved)

This is bean curd that has been preserved and flavoured with chilli, salt and spices. It is often cubed, comes in many flavours and white and red varieties are available. It is quite strong in flavour and is eaten on its own or used as a marinade, condiment or an accompaniment to congee. It can be found in glass jars in Chinese supermarkets.

Fermented salted black beans (dried)

These are small black soya beans that have been preserved in salt and so they must be rinsed in cold water before use. A common ingredient, they are used to make black bean sauce and can be found in Chinese supermarkets.

Fish ball/Fish cake (fresh)

The fleshy meat of white fish is combined with spices, salt and flour and made into fish balls or cakes, which are then fried or steamed and vacuum-packed ready to cook. Great added to stir-fries and soups. You can usually find many varieties in the Chinese supermarket with different flavourings, and you can also buy squid or cuttlefish balls, as well as vegetarian varieties.

Five-spice powder – see Chinese five-spice powder

Fresh bean curd (dofu/tofu) (fresh)

Described as the 'cheese' of China, fresh bean curd is made from protein-rich soya bean curd. It is white and quite bland, but takes on the flavour of whatever ingredients it is cooked with. It is used as a meat substitute in a vegetarian diet. In Japan it is called tofu and in Chinese, dofu. The texture is quite creamy and silky and there are various varieties, such as firm, soft and silken. The firm variety is great in soups, salads and stir-fries. Silken has a cream cheese-like texture. Dofu is protein-rich and contains B vitamins, isoflavones and calcium. The fresh variety is usually found in the chilled sections of Chinese supermarkets and can be kept chilled in the fridge for up to one week.

Gailan – see Chinese kale

Garlic chives (jiucai) (fresh)
Also known as Chinese chives, these have long, flat green leaves and a strong garlic flavour. There are two varieties, one with small yellow flowers at the top and one without. The flowers can be eaten. Both are delicious used in soups and stir-fries. Available from Chinese supermarkets.

Glutinous rice
Also called sticky rice, this is a short-grained rice that becomes sticky when cooked. It does not contain gluten. As an alternative, use sushi short-grain rice.

Groundnut oil (oil)
This pale oil is extracted from peanuts and has a subtle, nutty flavour. It can be heated to high temperatures without burning and is great to use in a salad dressing. As an alternative, use vegetable oil.

Hoisin sauce (sauce)
This is made from fermented soya beans, sugar, vinegar, star anise, sesame oil and red rice (which gives it a slight red colour). This is great used as a marinade and as a dipping sauce.

Jasmine rice (dried)
This is a long-grain white rice that originates from Thailand. The rice has a nutty jasmine-scented aroma and makes a delicious accompaniment to dishes. As with most rice, you need to rinse it before cooking until the water runs clear to get rid of any excess starch. White and silky, this rice when cooked is soft, white and fluffy.

Light soy sauce (condiment)
Light soy sauce is used in China instead of salt. It is made from fermented soya beans and wheat. A versatile and staple ingredient, it can be used in soups, stir-fries and braised and stewed dishes. Wheat-free varieties, called tamari, are available for those with wheat intolerance, and there are also low-sodium varieties for those watching their sodium intake.

Longjing tea (tea)
'Longjing' means 'Dragon well' and is the name of the area where this famous tea is grown in the Hangzhou region. A mild green (unfermented) tea, it has a gentle sweet flavour and a pure aroma. It is high in antioxidants and contains vitamin C and amino acids. Available at good tea shops, online, or from Chinese supermarkets.

Lychee (fruit)
Red or amber in colour, oval in shape and with a brittle skin, lychees are the fruit of an evergreen tree native to southern China. The translucent white or pinkish flesh is aromatic and has a distinctive flavour. In the centre is a largish seed. Available fresh or tinned.

Mijiu rice wine (condiment)
'Mi' means 'rice' and 'jiu' means 'wine'. A strong rice wine made from fermented glutinous rice, it is clear in colour and has a high alcoholic content, between 19% and 25%. Some varieties are sweet and served as a dessert liqueur. Great used in cooking, too. Can only be found in Chinese supermarkets. As an alternative, use vodka or gin.

Mung bean noodles (dried)
Made from the starch of green mung beans and water, these noodles come in various thicknesses. Vermicelli is the thinnest type. Soak in hot water for 5–6 minutes before cooking. If using in soups or deep-frying, no pre-soaking is necessary. They become translucent when cooked. Great in salads, stir-fries and soups, or even in spring rolls. Vermicelli rice noodles can be used as a substitute.

Oyster mushrooms (fresh)
This fungi is oyster-shaped, moist, hairless and fragrant, and comes in different colours – white, yellow and grey. It is soft and chewy with a slight oyster taste – great in a stir-fry.

Oyster sauce (sauce)
This seasoning sauce made from oyster extract originated in the Canton province in China. It is used liberally on vegetable dishes and can be used as a marinade. A vegetarian variety is also available. This is a very salty ingredient so taste the dish before adding.

Pak choy (fresh)
This is a vegetable from southern China. The broad green leaves, which taper to white stalks, are crisp and crunchy. It can be boiled, steamed or stir-fried.

Pickled chilli bamboo shoots (pickle)
Bamboo shoots that have been pickled in vinegar, salt and chilli oil. They're great when used to flavour soups and stir-fries. They can usually be found in glass jars in Chinese supermarkets.

Potato flour (ingredient)
Potatoes are steamed, dried and then ground to give this silky smooth white flour. It gives wonderful crispness to ingredients when they are coated in it before being shallow- or deep-fried. It is gluten free. Available from Chinese supermarkets and some supermarkets.

**Preserved mustard greens/
Pickled Chinese cabbage (pickle)**
The roots and leaves of the mustard
cabbage are preserved with plenty of
chilli and salt. They are available in
jars, tins or packets from Chinese
supermarkets.

Rambutans (fruit)
'Rambutan' is Malay for 'hairy' and
without the soft spines on its skin the
rambutan would resemble a lychee.
Tasting like a cross between a melon
and a lychee, the rambutan has an
inedible seed and white flesh and is
high in vitamin C. Fresh ripe
rambutans are mostly bright red in
colour. Available fresh or tinned.

Rice vinegar (condiment)
Plain rice vinegar is a clear vinegar
made from fermented rice. It is used in
dressings and for pickling and is more
common than black rice vinegar. Cider
vinegar can be used as a substitute.

Roasted soya beans (dried)
These are soya beans that have been
cooked and dry-roasted to give them
a crunchy texture. They're great as a
garnish. They can be bought ready to
eat from the health grain section of
supermarkets or in health food shops.
Alternatively, used dry-roasted peanuts.

Rock sugar (dried)
These large sugar crystals are slightly
golden-yellow in colour. They are used
like granulated sugar in Chinese
cooking. Use half the quantity of soft
brown sugar as a substitute.

Satay sauce (sauce)
Not to be confused with Thai peanut
satay sauce, this spicy salty sauce is
made from dried shrimps, chillies and
spices. This makes a great ingredient in a
stir-fry, or mix with soy sauce, chillies
and fresh herbs for a delicious dipping
sauce. Available from Chinese
supermarkets.

Sesame oil – see Toasted sesame oil

Sesame paste (paste)
This is made from crushed roasted
white sesame seeds blended with
toasted sesame oil to give a golden
brown paste, and is used with other
sauces to help flavour dishes. If you
cannot find this rich sesame paste, you
can use tahini (the Middle Eastern
equivalent) instead, but it is a lot lighter
in flavour and so you will need to add
more toasted sesame oil. Available from
Chinese supermarkets.

Sesame seeds (ingredient)
These oil-rich seeds come from an
annual plant, *Sesamum indicum*. They
add a nutty taste and a delicate texture
to many Asian dishes. Available in black,
white/yellow and red varieties, toasted
and untoasted.

Shaohsing rice wine (condiment)
This is wine made from rice, millet and
yeast, which has been aged for between
three and five years. Rice wine takes the
'odour' or 'rawness' out of meats and fish
and gives a bittersweet finish. Dry sherry
makes a good substitute.

Shi wheat flour noodles (dried)
'Shi' means 'thin/fine'. They are
available in white and yellow varieties.
The yellow variety has added colouring.
They're great in soups, salads and stir-
fries. Use egg noodles as a substitute.
Available from Chinese supermarkets.

Shiitake mushrooms (fresh)
These large dark-brown mushrooms are
umbrella-shaped fungi that are prized for
their culinary and medicinal properties.
They contain all eight essential amino
acids in more significant proportions
than soya beans, milk, meat and eggs, as
well as vitamins A, B, B12, C and D, niacin
and minerals. They are a staple in China,
Japan and other parts of Asia and are a
popular source of protein.

Sichuan chillies/dried chilli flakes
There are many different varieties of
Sichuan chillies – a common type is a
short, fat, bright red chilli that is hot and
fragrant. They are usually sun-dried. You
can grind the whole chillies in a pestle
and mortar to give flakes.

Sichuan peppercorns (spice)
Known as 'Hua jiao' in Mandarin or
'flower pepper', these are the outer pod
of a tiny fruit. They are widely used all
over China and especially in western
China. Can be wok-roasted, cooked in oil
to flavour the oil, or mixed with salt as a
condiment. They have a pungent citrusy
aroma.

Smoked paprika (spice)
Mild to red-hot peppers are smoke-dried
over wood and then ground to a powder.
The powder has a distinct flavour and
aroma. Sweet, hot and mild varieties are
available.

Snake beans (fresh)
Snake beans or long beans are mostly

grown in Asia. They are long, plump green beans, sometimes with a purple tinge to them, and since they are quite long, some varieties tend to twist. The fatter beans are more tender and sweet when cooked. This nutritious bean contains beta-carotene, vitamin C and phosphorus, and the Chinese use this plant to make tonics for ailing kidneys or for stomach problems. They make a great accompaniment to many dishes.

Spring roll wrappers/pastry (fresh)

Made from wheat flour and starch, these are used for wrapping foods such as spring rolls before deep-frying .Available in the frozen sections of Chinese supermarkets. If you can find the type made with coconut oil and salt, they can be eaten raw, filled with salad and with dressings. deep-fried or pan-fried. Filo pastry makes a good substitute.

Star anise (spice)

A staple ingredient in Chinese cooking, these are called 'Bajio' or 'eight horns' in Chinese. They are the fruit of a small evergreen plant that grows in southwest China. The star anise has an aniseed flavour and is one of the ingredients found in Chinese five-spice powder.

Thousand-year-old eggs (preserved)

These are duck eggs that have been buried in salt, tea leaves and rice husk, covered with sodium bicarbonate and left to mature for 40–50 days. The yolk has a rich creamy texture and, when served chilled, the white is clear, jelly-like and fragrant. Do not confuse these with preserved salted duck eggs – matured for 20 days, they have a deep orange yolk and an opaque clean white.

Toasted sesame oil (condiment)

Made from white pressed and toasted sesame seeds, this oil is used as a flavouring and is not suitable for use as a cooking oil since it burns easily. The flavour is intense, so use sparingly.

Tofu – see Fresh bean curd

Turmeric (spice)

This is a tuberous rhizome of the ginger family. The rhizomes are first cooked for several hours and then dried before being ground into a powder, deep yellow in colour. Turmeric imparts a strong yellow colour to any dish and gives a slightly mustardy, peppery, earthy flavour. It also has medicinal properties and is used for its antiseptic properties for cuts and burns.

Vermicelli mung bean noodles – see Mung bean noodles

Vermicelli rice noodle (dried)

Similar to vermicelli mung bean noodles, they come in many different widths and varieties. Soak in hot water for 5 minutes before cooking to soften. If using in salads, soak for 20 minutes. If using in a soup, add them dry. They turn opaque white when cooked. Great in soups, salads and stir-fries.

Wasabi (fresh/powder)

A Japanese variety of green horseradish, more fiery than the white. Combine wasabi powder with warm water to make a paste, or add warm cream.

Water chestnuts (tinned)

Water chestnuts are the roots of an aquatic plant that grows in freshwater ponds, marshes and lakes, and in slow-moving rivers and streams. Unpeeled, they resemble a chestnut in shape and colouring. They have a firm, crunchy texture. Sometimes available vacuum-packed, they are mostly sold in tins.

Wheat flour dumpling wrappers/ skins (fresh/frozen)

Made from wheat flour, water and salt, these are flat thin discs of finely rolled dough used to make dumplings. They can be found in the frozen or chilled sections of any Chinese supermarket. When using, keep covered with a damp towel to prevent them from drying out.

Wheat flour flat udon noodles (dried noodles)

This is a thin, white wheat flour noodle. Do not confuse these with the thick Japanese udon noodle. They are great in soups, salads and stir-fries.

Wheat flour pancakes (fresh)

Made from wheat flour, water and salt and rolled into very thin discs, these are steamed before serving and accompany Peking Duck and other dishes. They can be found in the frozen or chilled sections of any Chinese supermarket.

Wheat starch (dried)

Obtained from wheat grain. This white silken powder is combined with hot water and used to make dumpling skins that turn from opaque white to translucent white once steamed.

Wonton wrapper (fresh/frozen)

Made from egg, wheat flour, salt and water, they are used to make dumplings. They can be bought fresh or frozen from any Chinese supermarket.

Wood ear mushrooms – see Chinese wood ear mushrooms

Yellow bean sauce (sauce)

This is made from fermented yellow soya beans, dark brown sugar and rice wine. It makes a great marinade for meats and as a flavouring in many savoury dishes.

Notes for cooks

Buy organic produce when you can and, where possible, buy monosodium glutamate-free (MSG-free) condiments.

If you're watching your sodium intake, use a low-sodium soy sauce.

EGGS

Use medium eggs unless otherwise stated. Try to buy free-range and organic if possible.

CONVERSION CHARTS

g	oz	kg	lb	ml	fl oz	litres	pints
15	½	1	2¼	25	1	1	1¾
20	¾	1.1	2½	50	2		(1 quart US)
25	1	1.4	3	75	3	1.1	2
40	1½	1.6	3½	100	3½	1.7	3
50	2	1.8	4	125	4	2	3½
60	2½			150	5	2.3	4
75	3				(¼ pint)		
100	3½			175	6		
115	3¾			200	7		
125	4			225	8		
150	5				(1 cup US/		
175	6				Australia)		
200	7			250	9		
225	8			300	10		
250	9				(½ pint)		
275	10			325	11		
300	11			350	12		
320	11½			375	13		
350	12			400	14		
375	13			450	15		
400	14				(¾ pint)		
425	15			500	18		
450	1lb			600	20		
500	1lb 2oz				(1 pint)		
550	1lb 4oz			750	25		
600	1lb 5oz				(1¼ pints)		
650	1lb 6oz			900	30		
700	1½lb				(1½ pints)		
750	1lb 11oz						
800	1lb 12oz						
900	2lb						

MEASURING SPOONS

Teaspoons (5ml) and tablespoons (15ml) are the same in Britain as in the USA. Australian cooks should note that an Australian tablespoon (20ml) is larger than the British.

AMERICAN CUPS/CONVERSIONS

Increasingly, American cooks are investing in scales, which make measuring more accurate. If using American cups, here are the most common translations.

Butter	225g/8oz	1 cup/2 sticks
Flour	150g/5oz	1 cup
Nuts, chopped	125g/4oz	1 cup
Rice	200g/7oz	1 cup
Sugar	200g/7oz	1 cup

One US pint = 16fl oz (475ml); one UK pint = 20fl oz (600ml).

UK TERM	US TERM	UK TERM	US TERM
aubergine	eggplant	iceberg lettuce	crisphead lettuce
baking tray	cookie sheet	icing sugar	confectioners' sugar
caster sugar	superfine sugar	kitchen paper	paper towel
clingfilm	plastic wrap	mandarin	mandarin orange
coriander	cilantro	minced pork/beef	ground pork/beef
cornflour	cornstarch	pak choy	bok choy
courgette	zucchini	pan/frying pan	skillet
double cream	heavy cream	plain flour	all-purpose flour
edamame bean	young soya bean	prawns	shrimp
French bean	green bean	soda water	club soda
fresh root ginger	green ginger	spring onion	scallion
gelatine granules	unflavored gelatine	spring roll	egg roll
golden syrup	light corn syrup	stone	pit
greaseproof paper	waxed paper	tiger prawn	jumbo shrimp
green/red/yellow pepper	bell/sweet pepper	wonton wrappers	wonton skins
groundnut oil	peanut oil	wood ear mushroom	cloud ear mushroom
ham	cured pig meat		

Index

ACKNOWLEDGEMENTS

I am so grateful to everyone who has inspired, supported and believed in me, to have allowed me to progress and develop. This book would not have been possible without my commissioning editor, Vivien Bowler, and my agent, Jeremy Hicks. Thank you so much for believing in me and for making this happen. I am very honoured and privileged to be working with you both. I am so fortunate to have an amazing talented team – Kate Whitaker (photographer) for her professional amazing eye, Annie Nichols (stylist) for the fabulous food presentation, and Wei Tang (props stylist) for choosing the gorgeous pieces and designs, allowing us to show off the food so beautifully. Thanks to Barbara Dixon, my editor, for keeping such a level head and for working through all the details when I was myself hazy, and to Jacqui Caulton, the talented designer, for bringing it all together – I am indebted. There is an enormous amount of detail that goes into the production of such a book and I am so grateful to everyone for making it so beautiful – I cannot thank you all enough.

To all the people who are helping to shape my TV career, thank you for continuing to give me opportunities; it means so much to me that you enjoy my food and it has been wonderful working with you all. In particular, Jeremy Mills and Richard Shaw at Lion TV and, of course, all the big bosses and powers-that-be at the BBC for making *Chinese Food Made Easy* a reality. Thank you for allowing me the pleasure of sharing my food with the British public. My deepest thanks from my heart to you all for your faith, support and encouragement. I wish you all 'Chong sheng ping an' and 'Wan shi ruyi'. To the team – David Robertson (you're a real gem), Katharine Ibbs-Westmore (a true professional), Gillian Pauling, Anna Greenaway, Jaime Brannan, Tom Hayward, Chris Youle-Grayling, Gillian Pauling, Annina Vogel, Hugh Hughes and Matt Champion – I have learnt so much from you all.

To all my customers, I'm sorry if I've neglected you over these past months! Thanks for your understanding, for keeping my business going and for supporting what we do at Fuge. To all my staff at Fuge, and in particular Jesslyn Wong, thank you for coping without me – this book would not have been possible without you.

To my friends and family – thank you for your support, love and care. To my Sao Sao and brother, who have helped me more than I can express. To Jamie Cho, thank you for being there and for being my 'bodyguard' and companion during our travels together. To my parents – I am so lucky to have you both and we have been through stormy seas together these last ten years but I can now slowly see the sunlight. To my grandmother and mother, thank you for all the meals you have cooked for me – the labour of your love for us.

To my Buddhist masters, Cheng-yen (Tzu-Chi Charity) and Khenpo Karma Jigme, thank you for your continued guidance, blessing and teachings from your heart, they continue to inspire and enrich me.

BIBLIOGRAPHY

These books have been really useful in my research for this book:

A Cook's Guide to Asian Vegetables, Wendy Hutton, Periplus editions, 2004

Asian Sauces and Marinades, Wendy Sweetser, Firefly books Ltd, 2002

China Modern, Ching-He Huang, Kyle Cathie, 2006

Food in Chinese Culture – anthropological and historical perspectives, Edited by K.C. Chang, SMC Publishing Inc, Taipei, 1977

The Chinese Kitchen, Eileen Yin-Fei Lo, William Morrow and Co, 1999

The Chinese Kitchen, Deh-Ta Hsiung, Kyle Cathie, 2006

The Forbidden City, Great Wall Publishing Group, 2005

The Oxford Companion to Food, Alan Davidson, Oxford University Press, 1999

Yan Kit So's Classic Chinese Cookbook, Dorling Kindersley, London, 1984